WAR OF STREETS AND HOUSES

Also by Sophie Yanow:

In Situ (Colosse, 2011-2013)

Sleepy Details (Colosse)

The French Canadian edition of this work, titled *La guerre des rues et des maisons*, is published by la mauvaise tête, under the direction of Sébastien Trahan and Vincent Giard.

Design & Editing by Tom Kaczynski & Sophie Yanow
Production assistant Joel McKeen

Uncivilized Books
P.O. Box 6434
Minneapolis, MN 55406
USA
uncivilizedbooks.com

First American Edition, April 2014
Second American Edition, October 2015

10 9 8 7 6 5 4 3 2

ISBN 978-0-9846814-8-8

DISTRIBUTED TO THE TRADE BY:

Consortium Book Sales & Distribution, LLC.
34 Thirteenth Avenue NE,
Suite 101 Minneapolis,
MN 55413-1007
Orders: (800) 283-3572

Printed in USA

WAR OF STREETS AND HOUSES

SOPHIE YANOW

UNCIVILIZED BOOKS, PUBLISHER

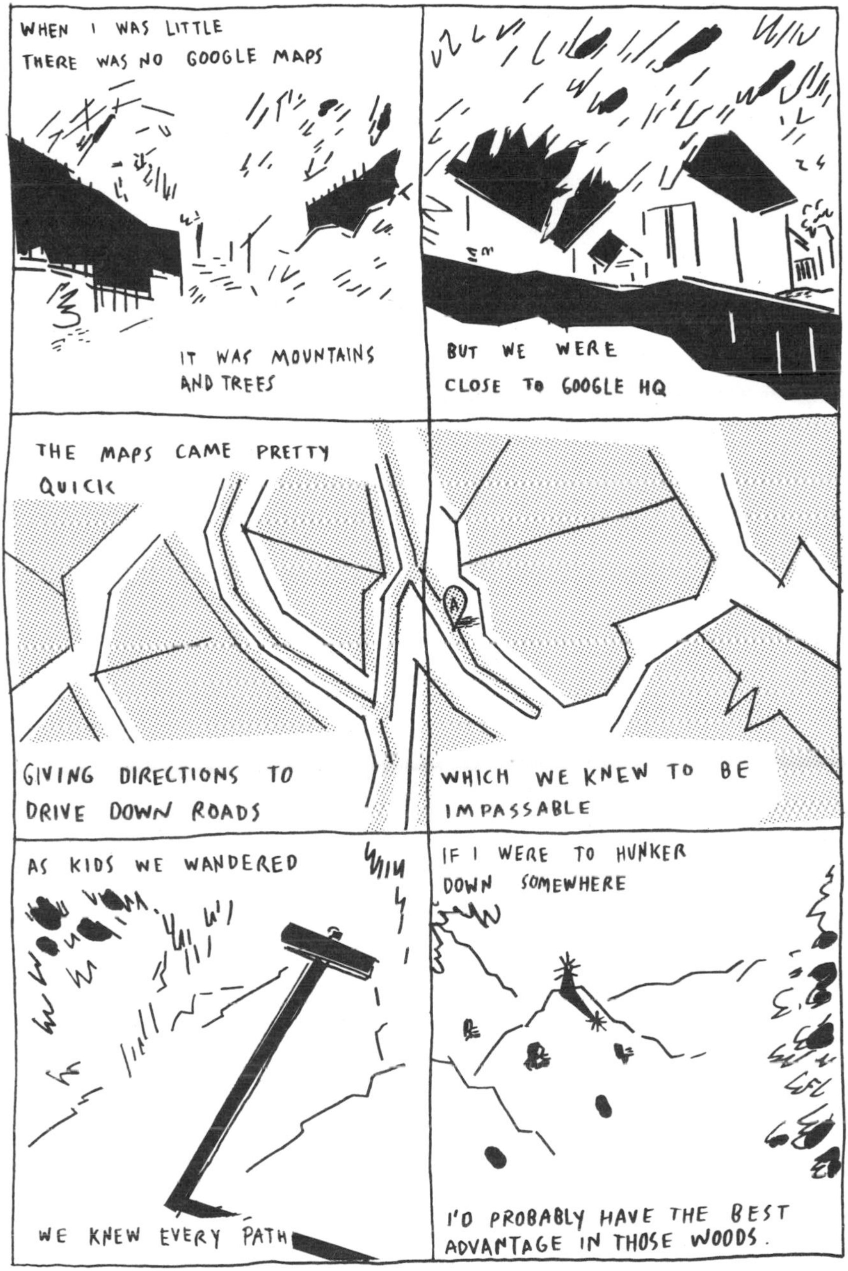
WHEN I WAS LITTLE
THERE WAS NO GOOGLE MAPS
IT WAS MOUNTAINS AND TREES
BUT WE WERE CLOSE TO GOOGLE HQ
THE MAPS CAME PRETTY QUICK
GIVING DIRECTIONS TO DRIVE DOWN ROADS
WHICH WE KNEW TO BE IMPASSABLE
AS KIDS WE WANDERED
WE KNEW EVERY PATH
IF I WERE TO HUNKER DOWN SOMEWHERE
I'D PROBABLY HAVE THE BEST ADVANTAGE IN THOSE WOODS.

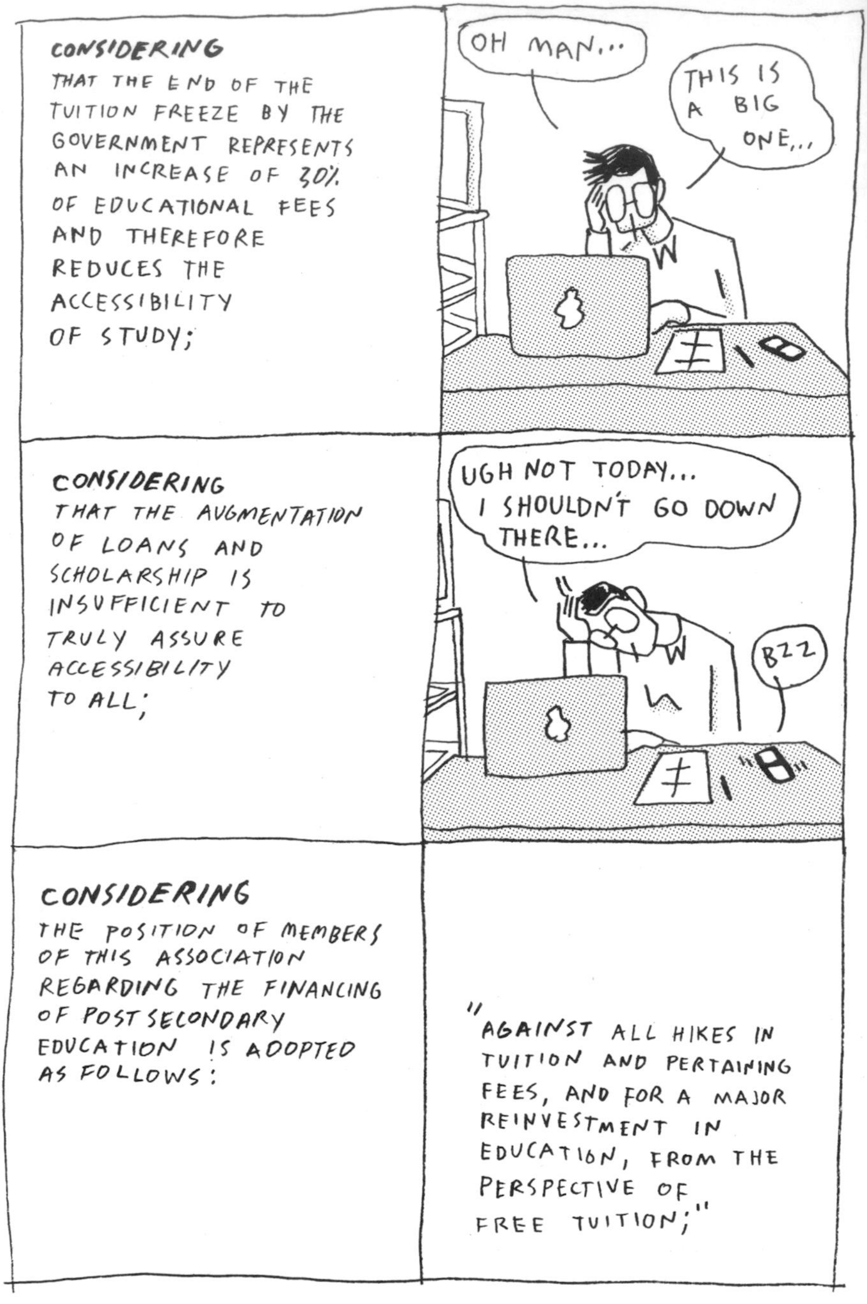
CONSIDERING
THAT THE END OF THE TUITION FREEZE BY THE GOVERNMENT REPRESENTS AN INCREASE OF 30% OF EDUCATIONAL FEES AND THEREFORE REDUCES THE ACCESSIBILITY OF STUDY;
OH MAN...
THIS IS A BIG ONE...
CONSIDERING
THAT THE AUGMENTATION OF LOANS AND SCHOLARSHIP IS INSUFFICIENT TO TRULY ASSURE ACCESSIBILITY TO ALL;
UGH NOT TODAY... I SHOULDN'T GO DOWN THERE...
BZZ
CONSIDERING
THE POSITION OF MEMBERS OF THIS ASSOCIATION REGARDING THE FINANCING OF POST SECONDARY EDUCATION IS ADOPTED AS FOLLOWS:
"AGAINST ALL HIKES IN TUITION AND PERTAINING FEES, AND FOR A MAJOR REINVESTMENT IN EDUCATION, FROM THE PERSPECTIVE OF FREE TUITION;"

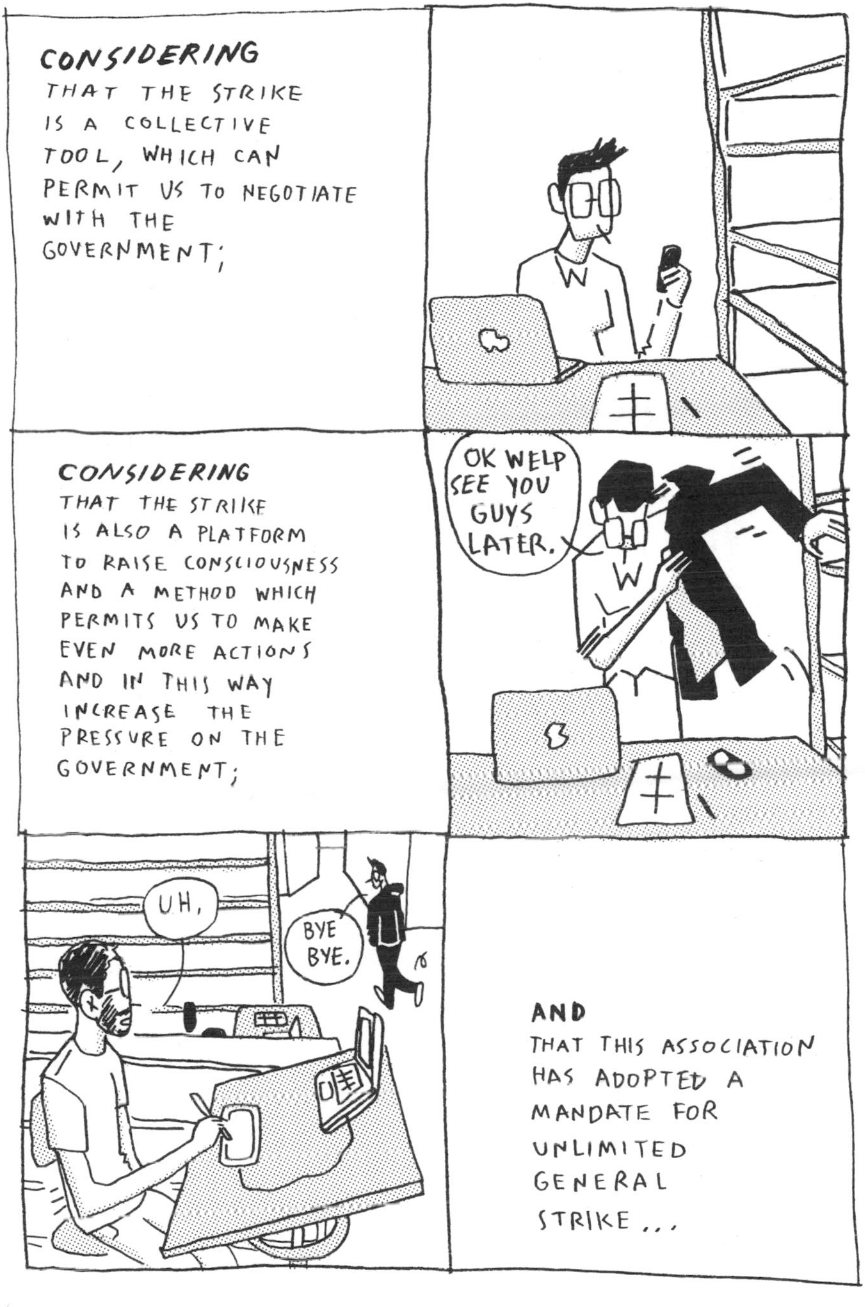
CONSIDERING
THAT THE STRIKE IS A COLLECTIVE TOOL, WHICH CAN PERMIT US TO NEGOTIATE WITH THE GOVERNMENT;
CONSIDERING
THAT THE STRIKE IS ALSO A PLATFORM TO RAISE CONSCIOUSNESS AND A METHOD WHICH PERMITS US TO MAKE EVEN MORE ACTIONS AND IN THIS WAY INCREASE THE PRESSURE ON THE GOVERNMENT;
OK WELP SEE YOU GUYS LATER.
UH,
BYE BYE.
AND
THAT THIS ASSOCIATION HAS ADOPTED A MANDATE FOR UNLIMITED GENERAL STRIKE...

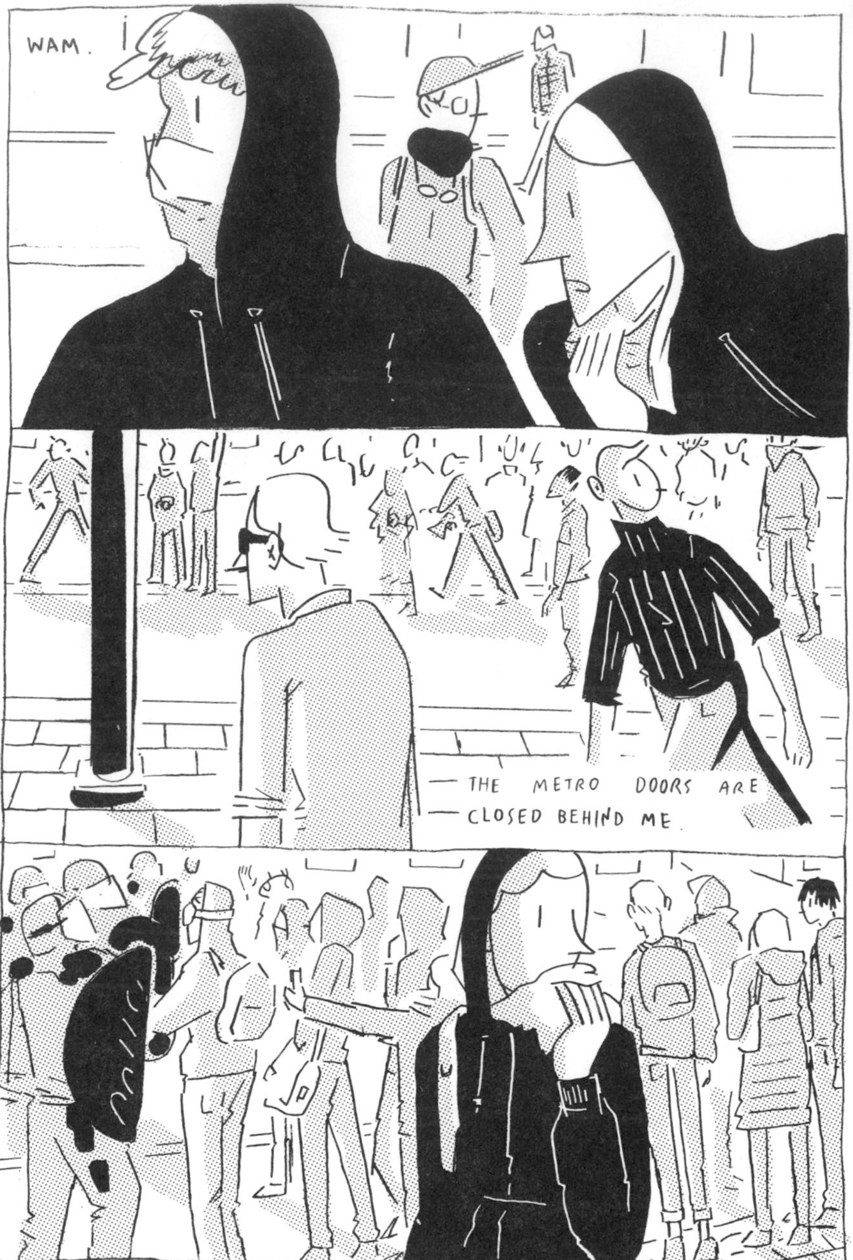
WAM.
THE METRO DOORS ARE CLOSED BEHIND ME.

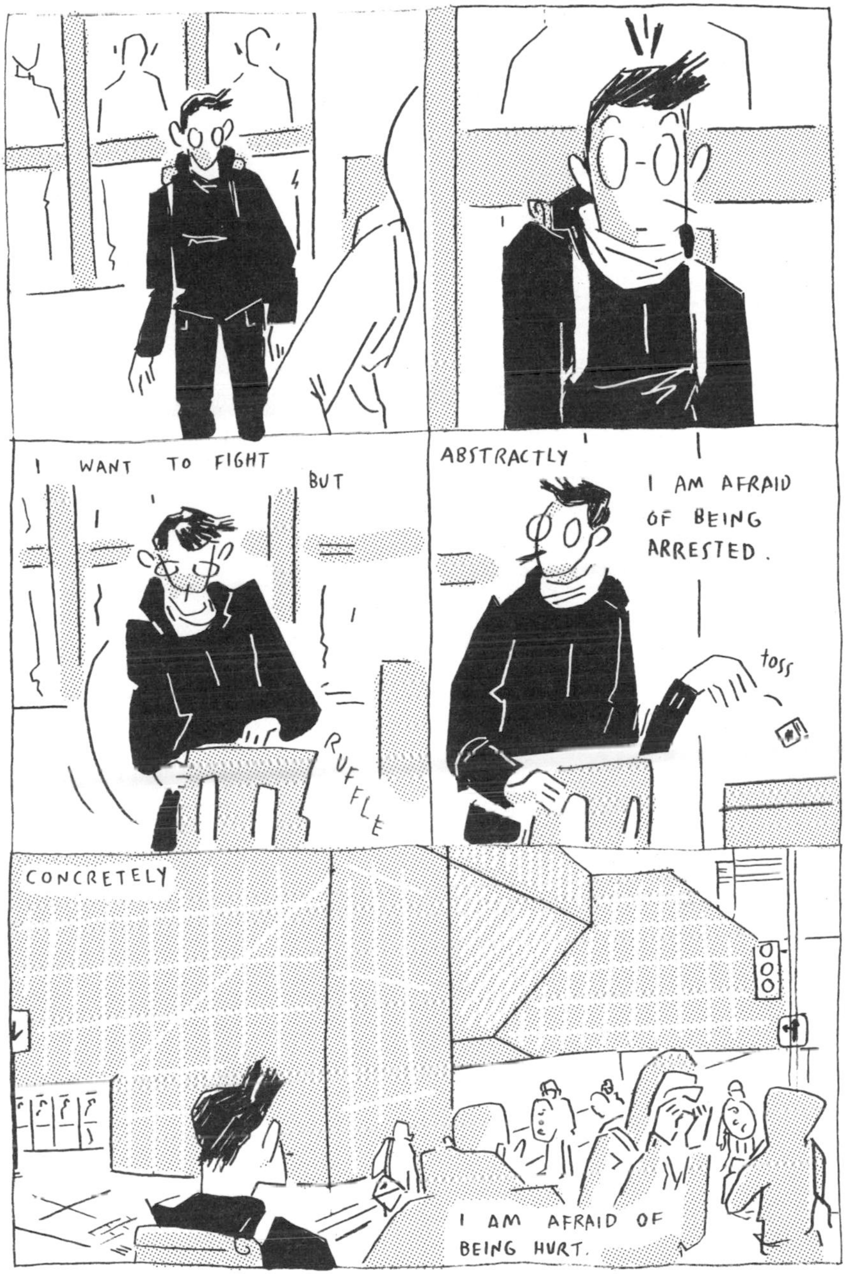
I WANT TO FIGHT
BUT
RUFFLE
ABSTRACTLY
I AM AFRAID OF BEING ARRESTED.
toss
CONCRETELY
I AM AFRAID OF BEING HURT.

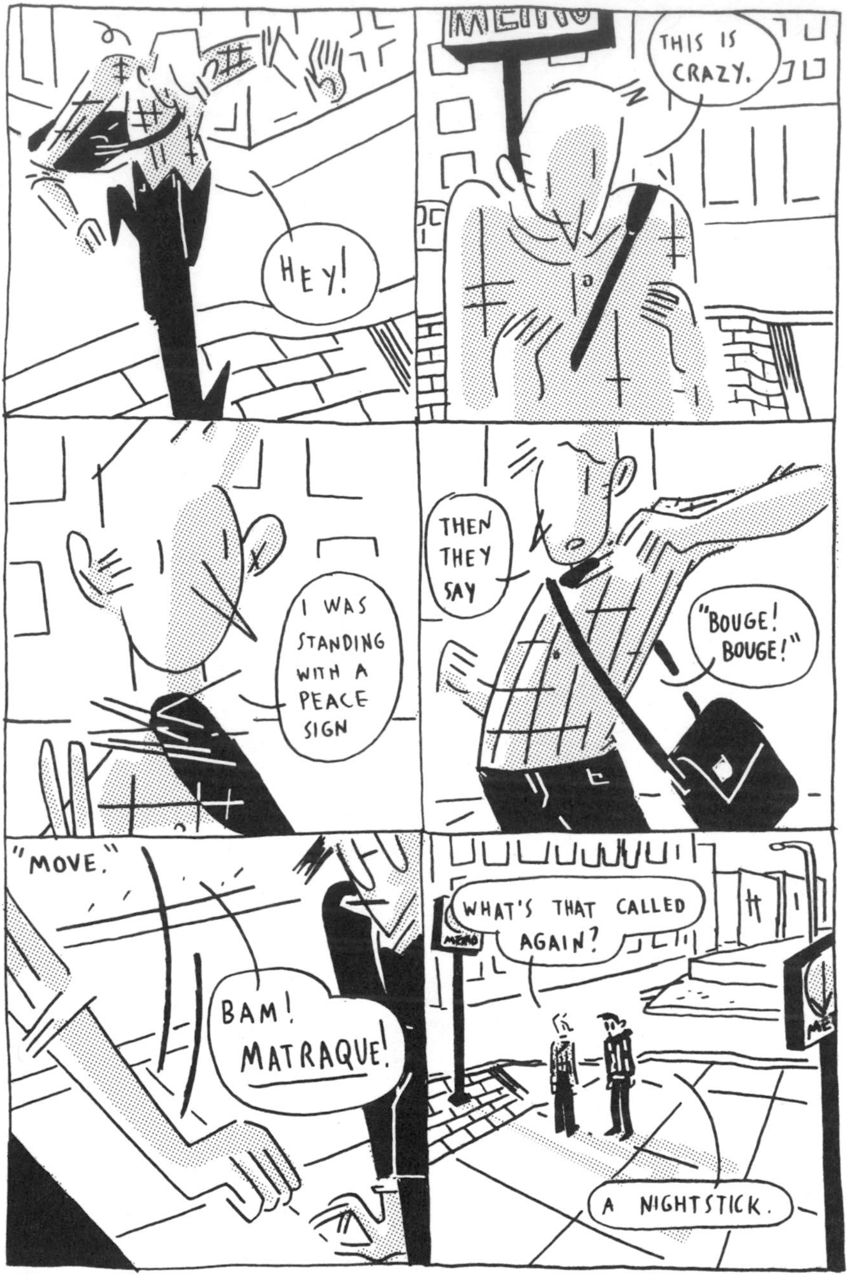
HEY!
THIS IS CRAZY.
I WAS STANDING WITH A PEACE SIGN
THEN THEY SAY
"BOUGE! BOUGE!"
"MOVE."
BAM! MATRAQUE!
WHAT'S THAT CALLED AGAIN?
A NIGHTSTICK.

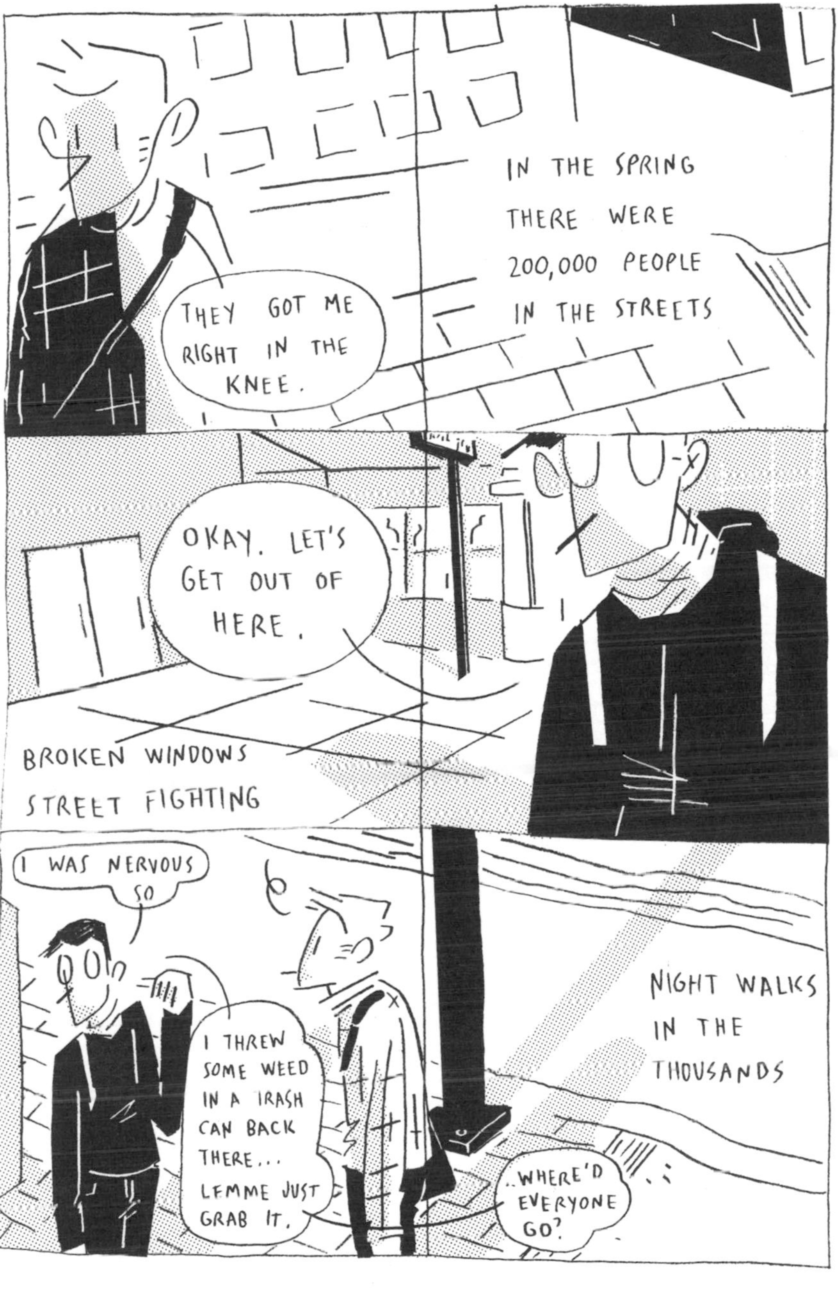
THEY GOT ME RIGHT IN THE KNEE.
IN THE SPRING THERE WERE 200,000 PEOPLE IN THE STREETS
OKAY. LET'S GET OUT OF HERE.
BROKEN WINDOWS STREET FIGHTING
I WAS NERVOUS SO
I THREW SOME WEED IN A TRASH CAN BACK THERE... LEMME JUST GRAB IT.
NIGHT WALKS IN THE THOUSANDS
..WHERE'D EVERYONE GO?

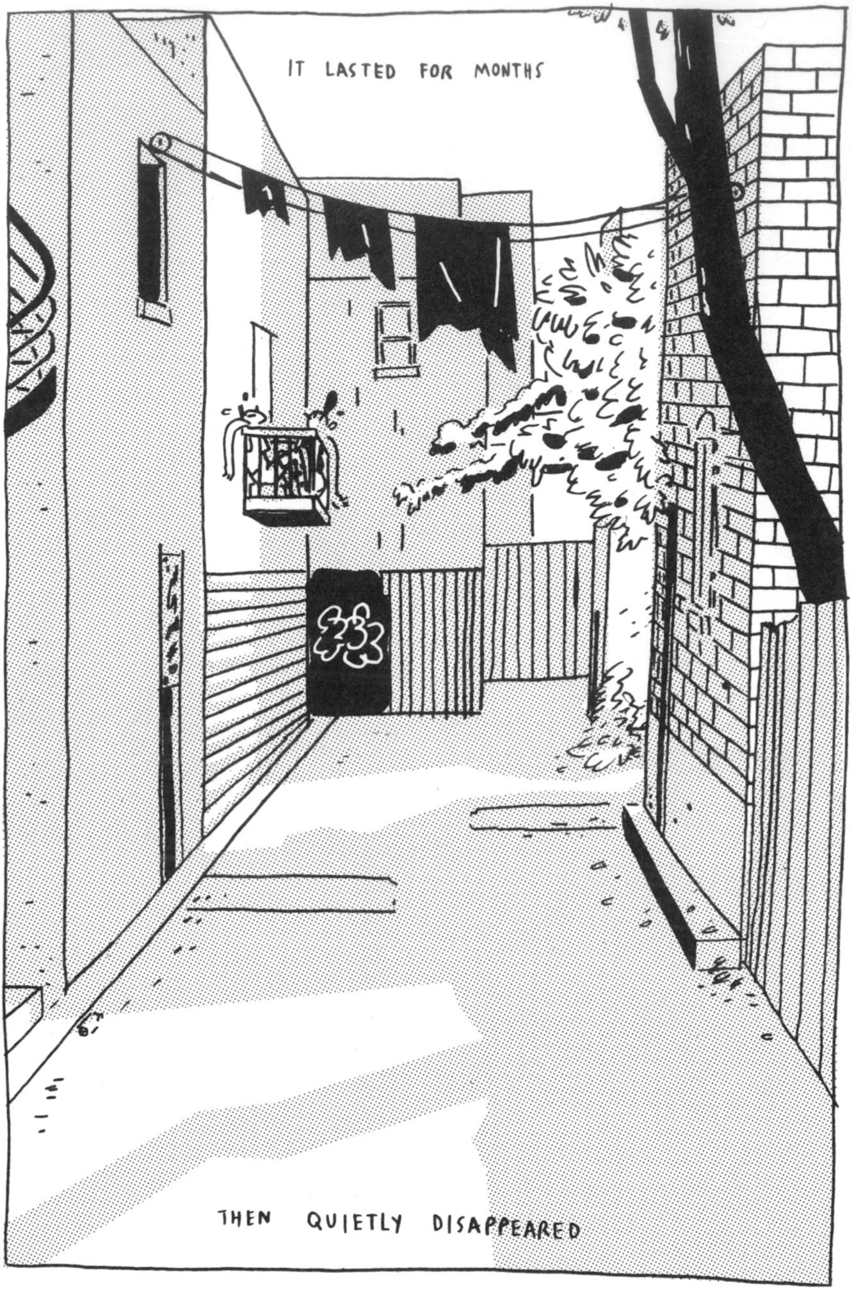
IT LASTED FOR MONTHS
THEN QUIETLY DISAPPEARED

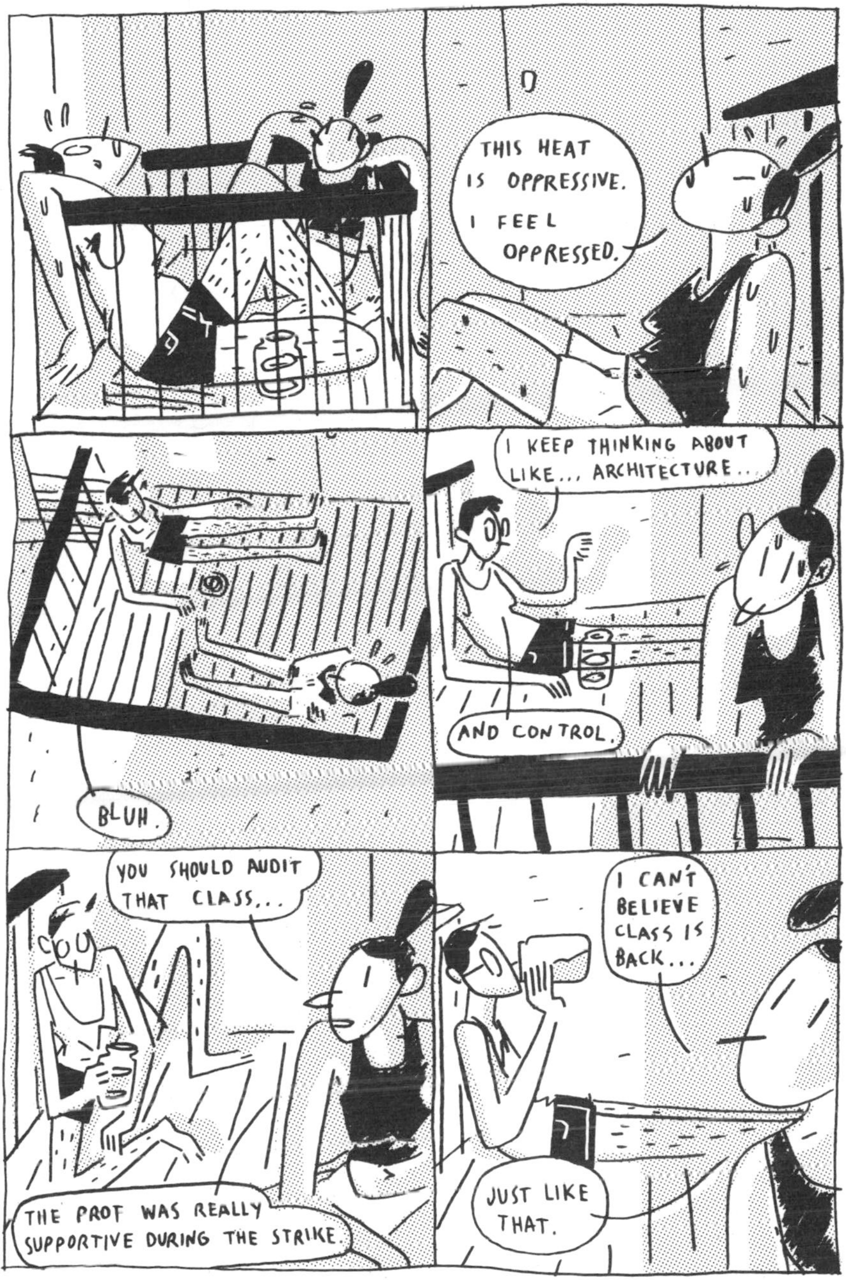
THIS HEAT IS OPPRESSIVE. I FEEL OPPRESSED.
I KEEP THINKING ABOUT LIKE... ARCHITECTURE...
AND CONTROL.
BLUH.
YOU SHOULD AUDIT THAT CLASS...
THE PROF WAS REALLY SUPPORTIVE DURING THE STRIKE.
I CAN'T BELIEVE CLASS IS BACK...
JUST LIKE THAT.

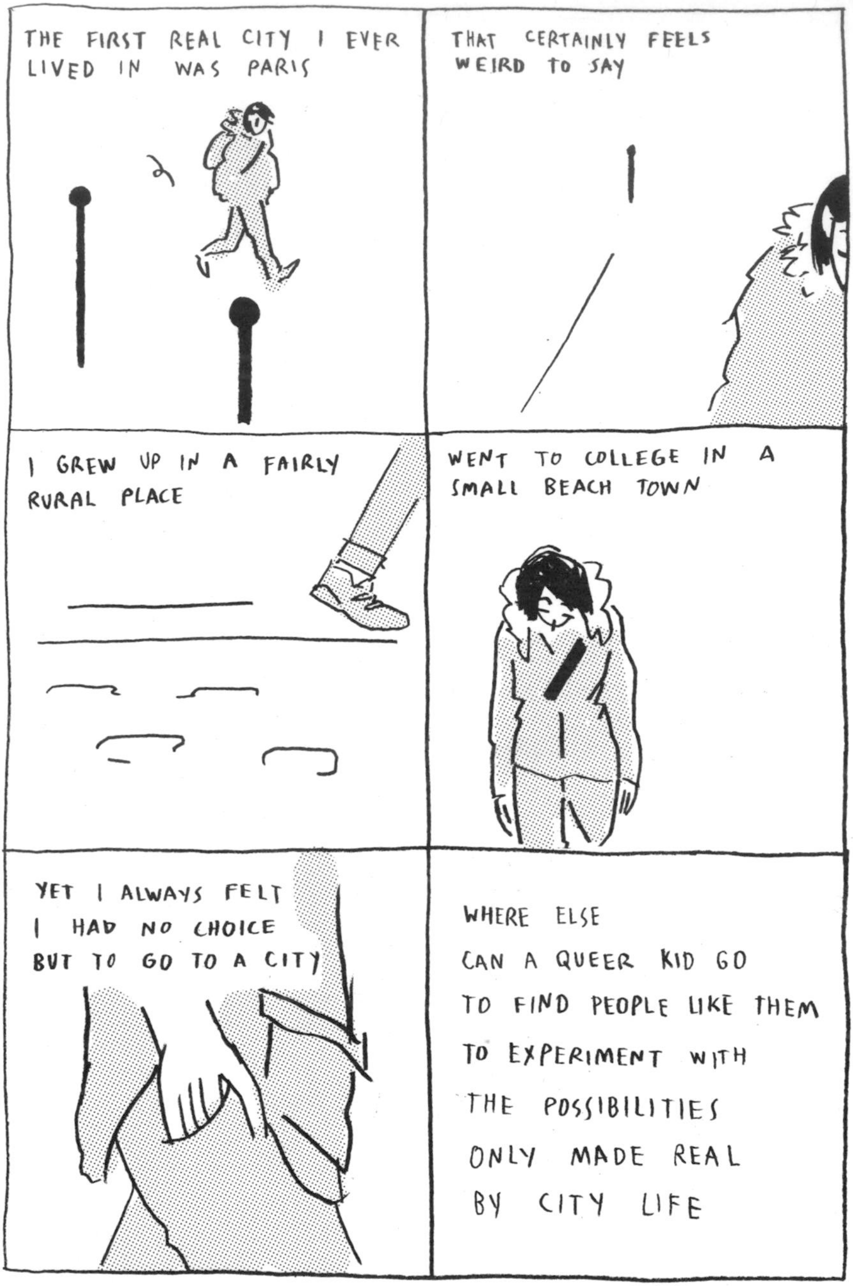
THE FIRST REAL CITY I EVER LIVED IN WAS PARIS
THAT CERTAINLY FEELS WEIRD TO SAY
I GREW UP IN A FAIRLY RURAL PLACE
WENT TO COLLEGE IN A SMALL BEACH TOWN
YET I ALWAYS FELT I HAD NO CHOICE BUT TO GO TO A CITY
WHERE ELSE
CAN A QUEER KID GO
TO FIND PEOPLE LIKE THEM
TO EXPERIMENT WITH
THE POSSIBILITIES
ONLY MADE REAL
BY CITY LIFE

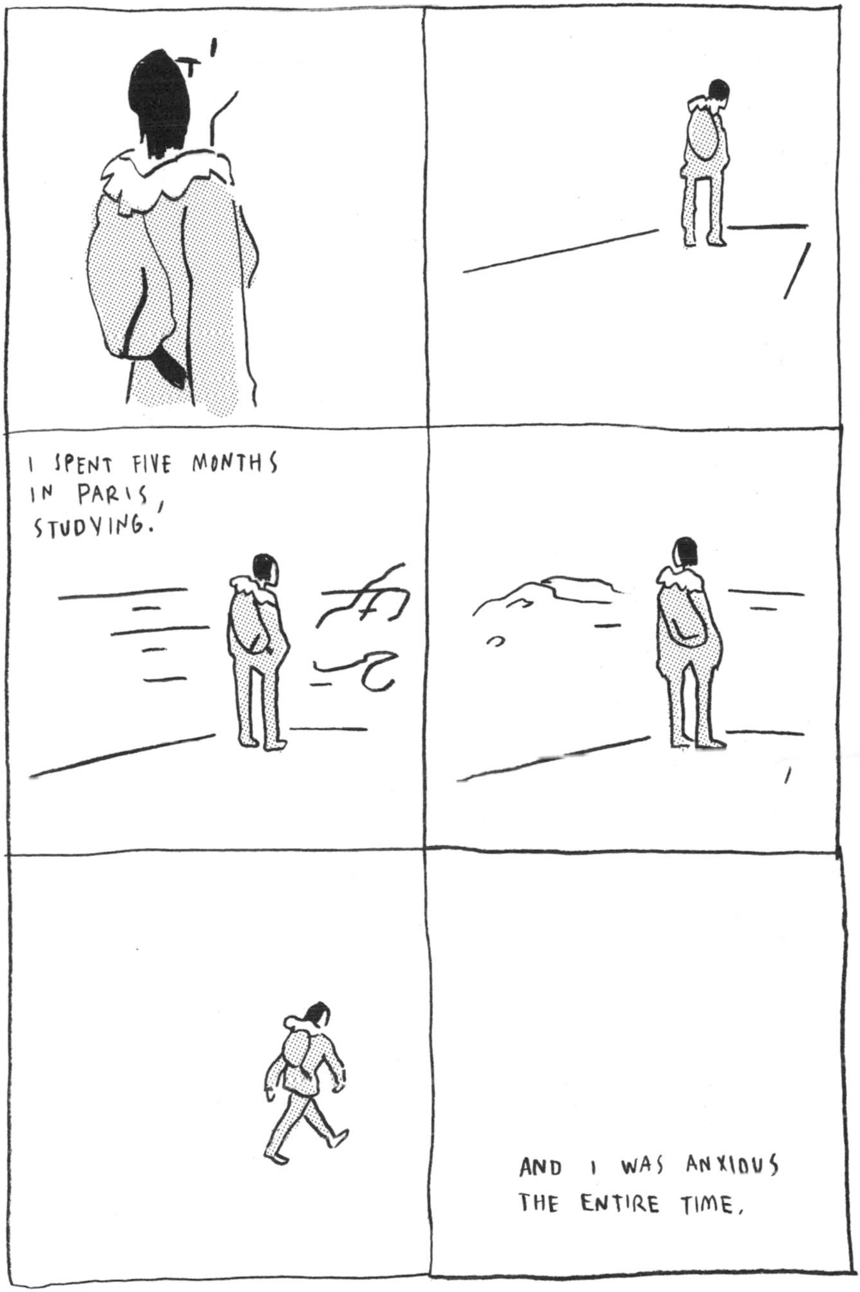
I SPENT FIVE MONTHS IN PARIS, STUDYING.
AND I WAS ANXIOUS THE ENTIRE TIME.

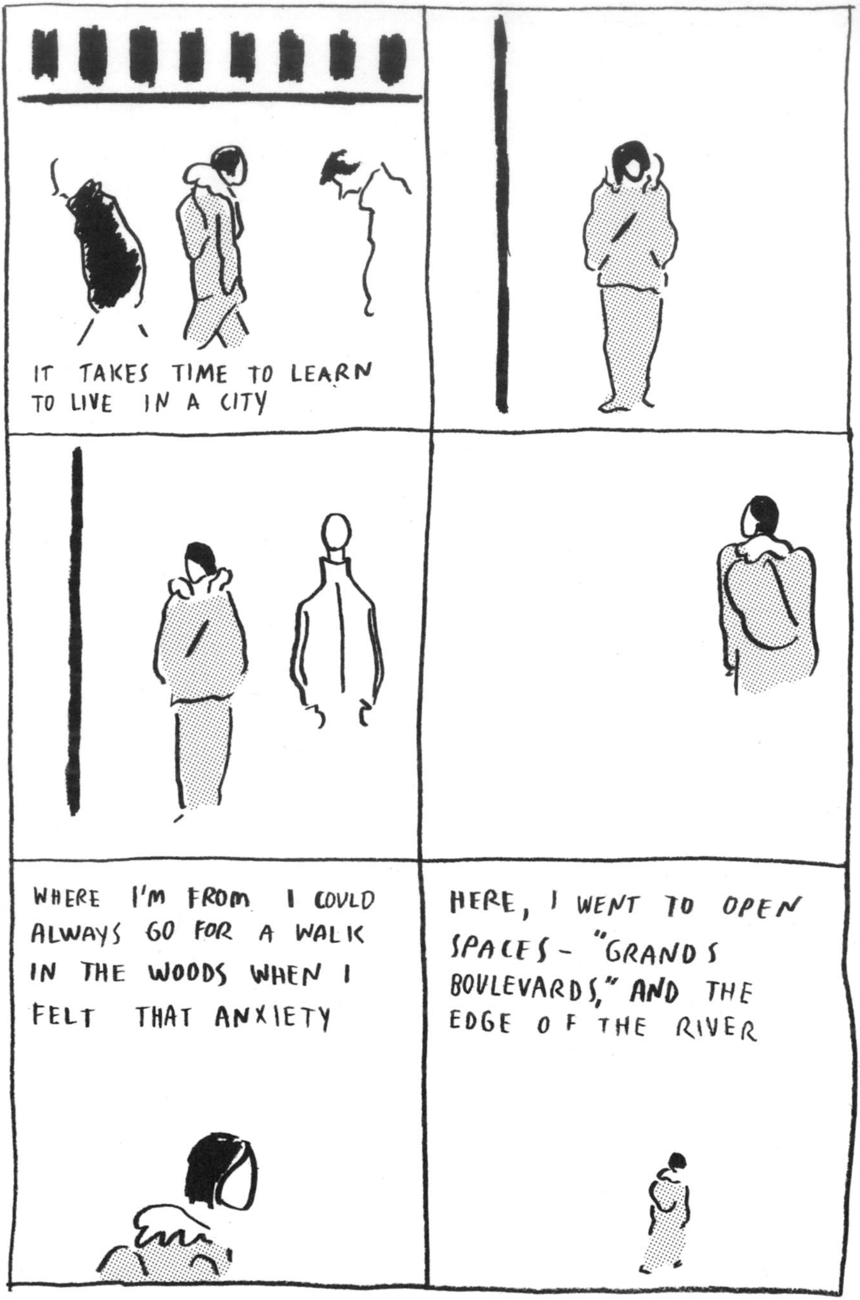
IT TAKES TIME TO LEARN TO LIVE IN A CITY
WHERE I'M FROM I COULD ALWAYS GO FOR A WALK IN THE WOODS WHEN I FELT THAT ANXIETY
HERE, I WENT TO OPEN SPACES - "GRANDS BOULEVARDS," AND THE EDGE OF THE RIVER

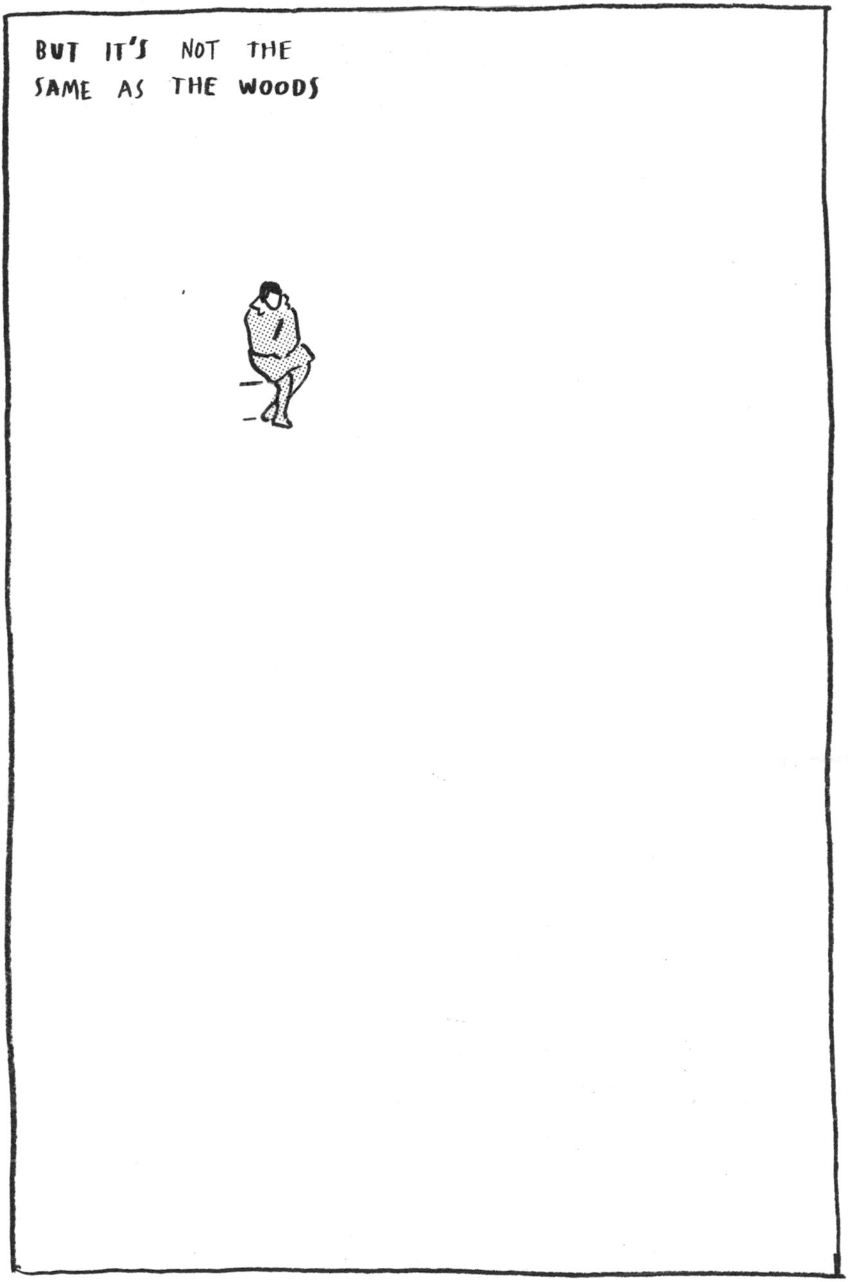
BUT IT'S NOT THE
SAME AS THE WOODS

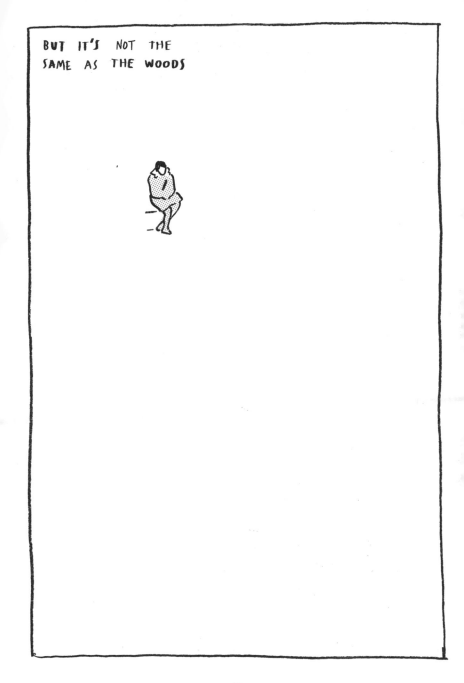

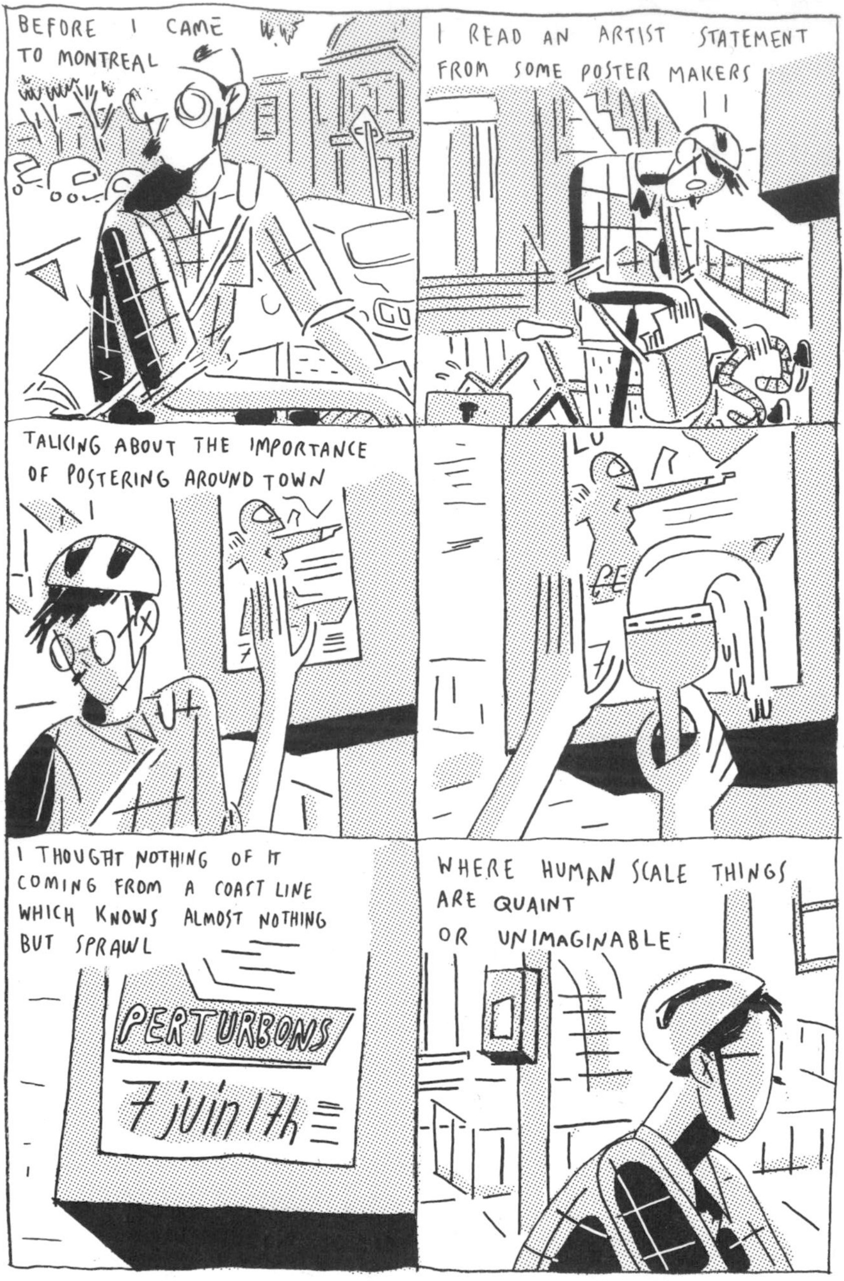
BEFORE I CAME TO MONTREAL
I READ AN ARTIST STATEMENT FROM SOME POSTER MAKERS
TALKING ABOUT THE IMPORTANCE OF POSTERING AROUND TOWN
I THOUGHT NOTHING OF IT COMING FROM A COAST LINE WHICH KNOWS ALMOST NOTHING BUT SPRAWL
PERTURBONS
7 juin 17h
WHERE HUMAN SCALE THINGS ARE QUAINT OR UNIMAGINABLE

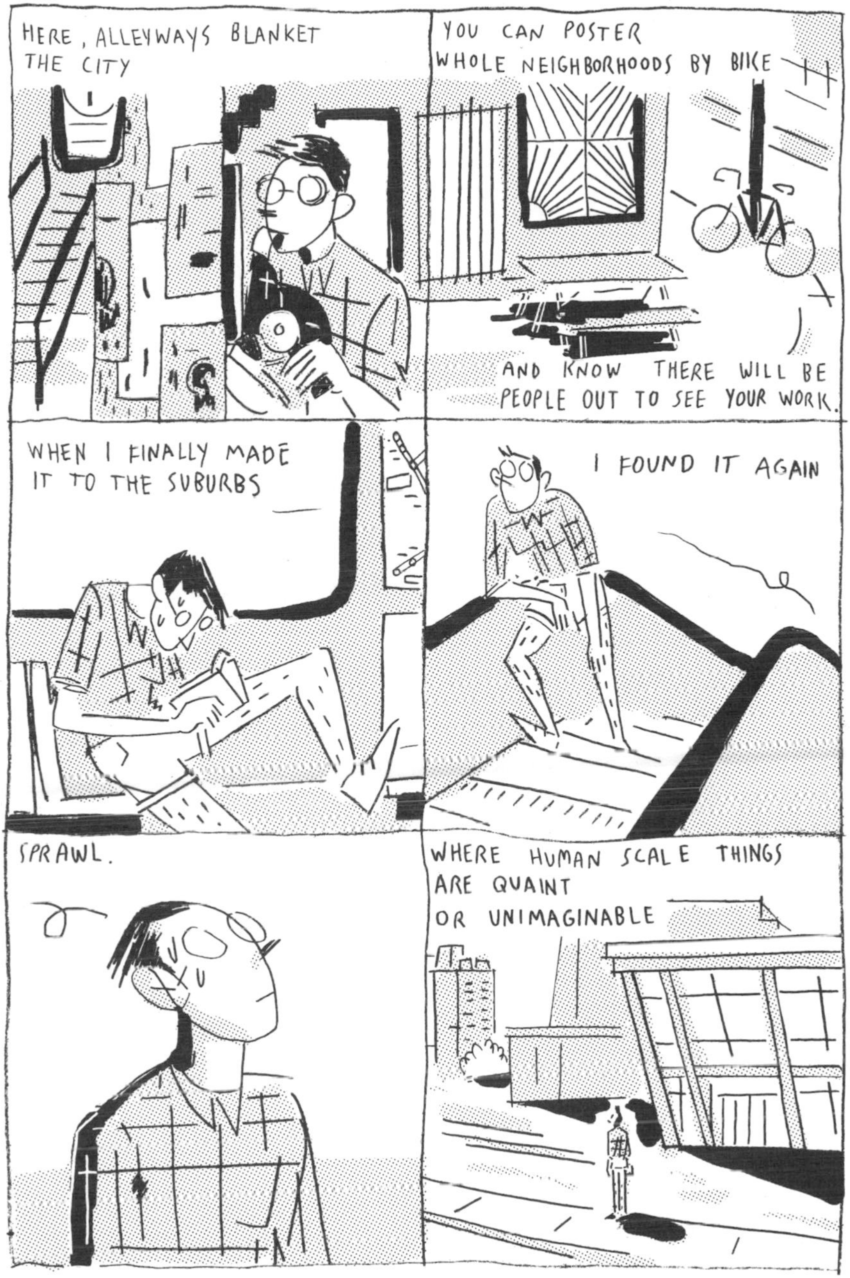
HERE, ALLEYWAYS BLANKET THE CITY
YOU CAN POSTER WHOLE NEIGHBORHOODS BY BIKE
AND KNOW THERE WILL BE PEOPLE OUT TO SEE YOUR WORK.
WHEN I FINALLY MADE IT TO THE SUBURBS
I FOUND IT AGAIN
SPRAWL.
WHERE HUMAN SCALE THINGS ARE QUAINT
OR UNIMAGINABLE

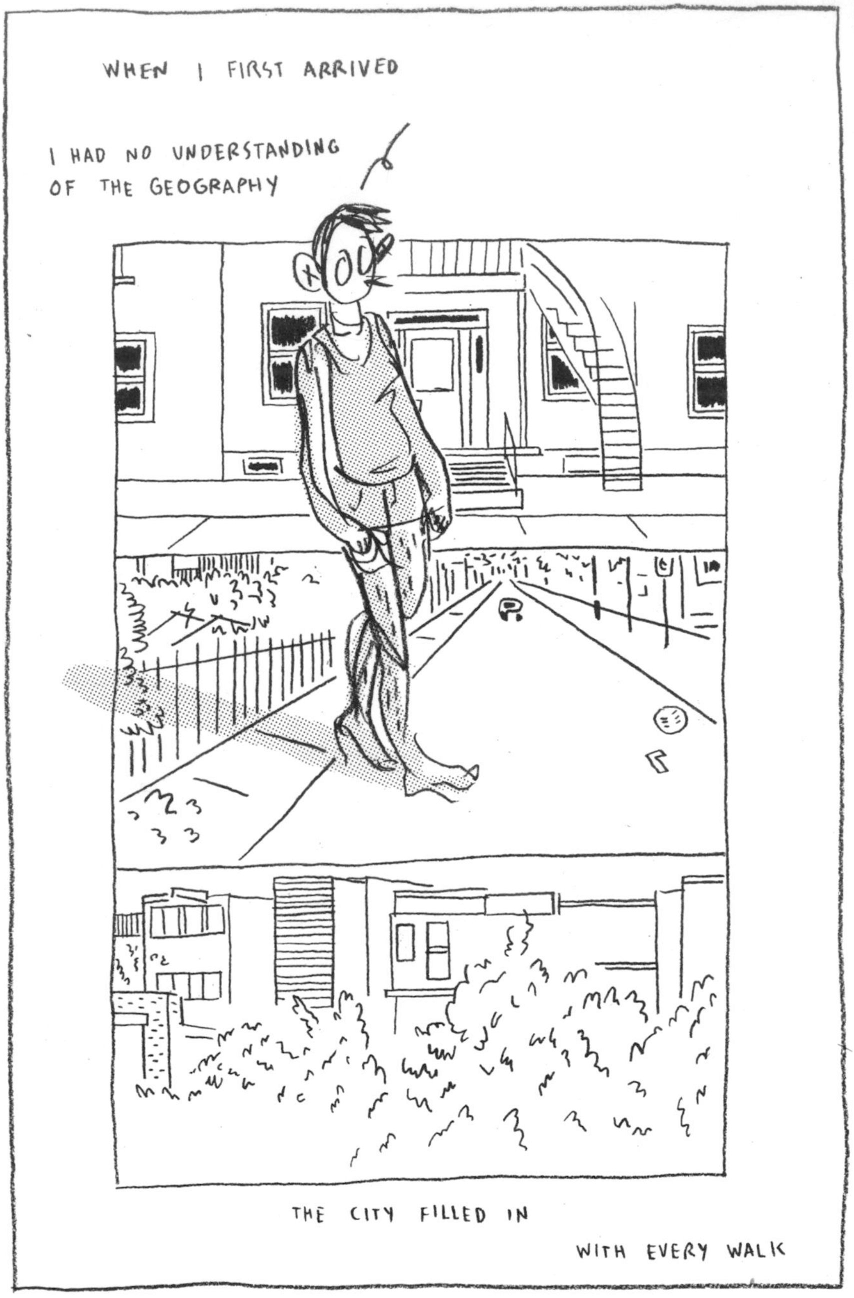
WHEN I FIRST ARRIVED
I HAD NO UNDERSTANDING OF THE GEOGRAPHY
THE CITY FILLED IN
WITH EVERY WALK

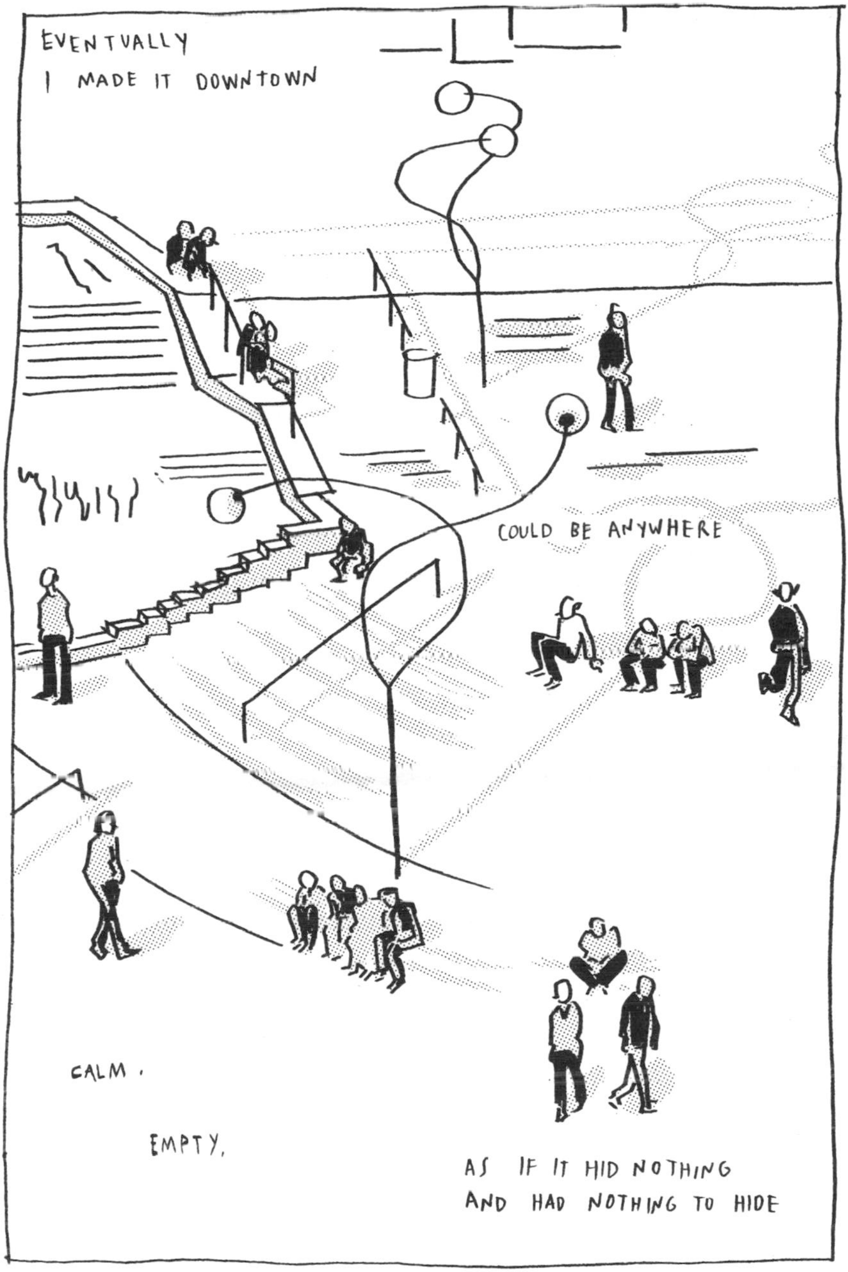
EVENTUALLY
I MADE IT DOWNTOWN
COULD BE ANYWHERE
CALM.
EMPTY,
AS IF IT HID NOTHING
AND HAD NOTHING TO HIDE

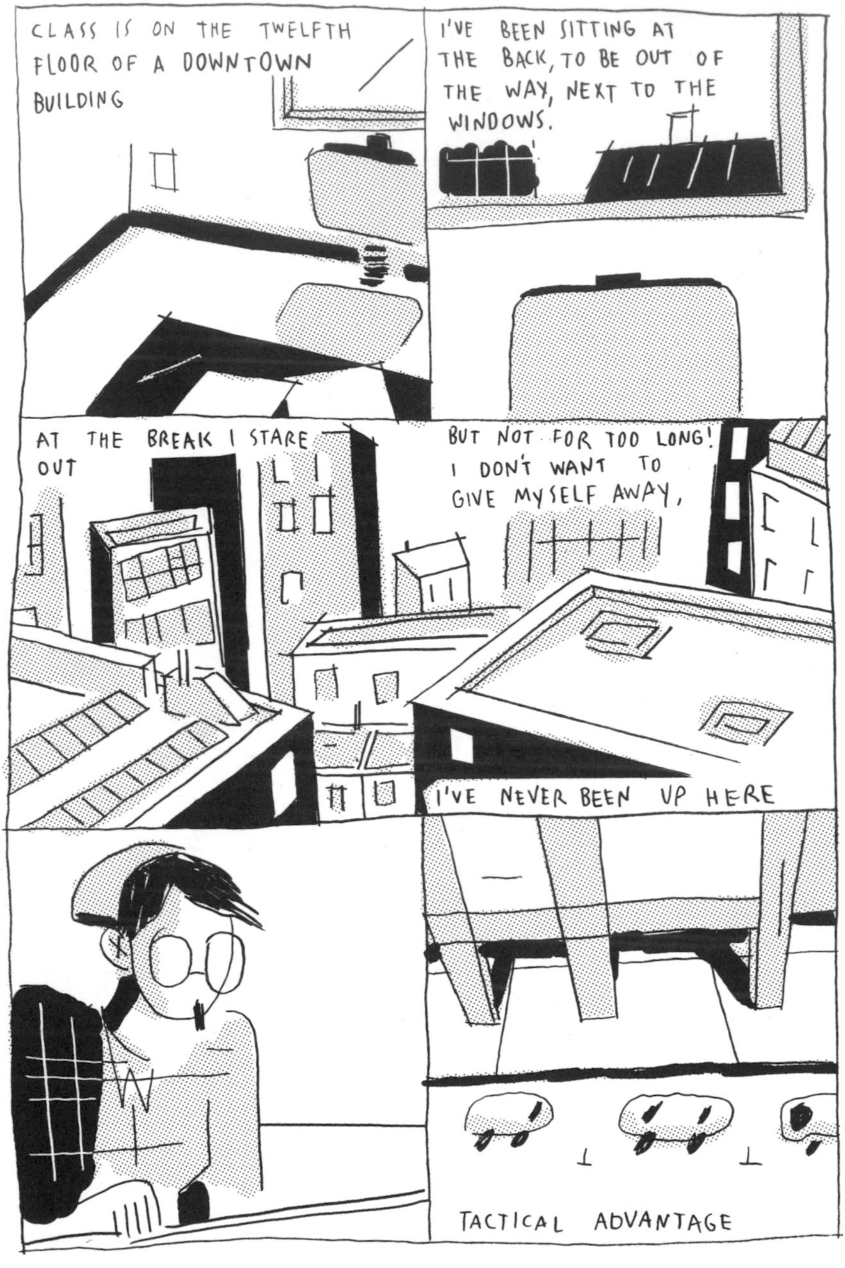
CLASS IS ON THE TWELFTH FLOOR OF A DOWNTOWN BUILDING
I'VE BEEN SITTING AT THE BACK, TO BE OUT OF THE WAY, NEXT TO THE WINDOWS.
AT THE BREAK I STARE OUT
BUT NOT FOR TOO LONG! I DON'T WANT TO GIVE MYSELF AWAY,
I'VE NEVER BEEN UP HERE
TACTICAL ADVANTAGE

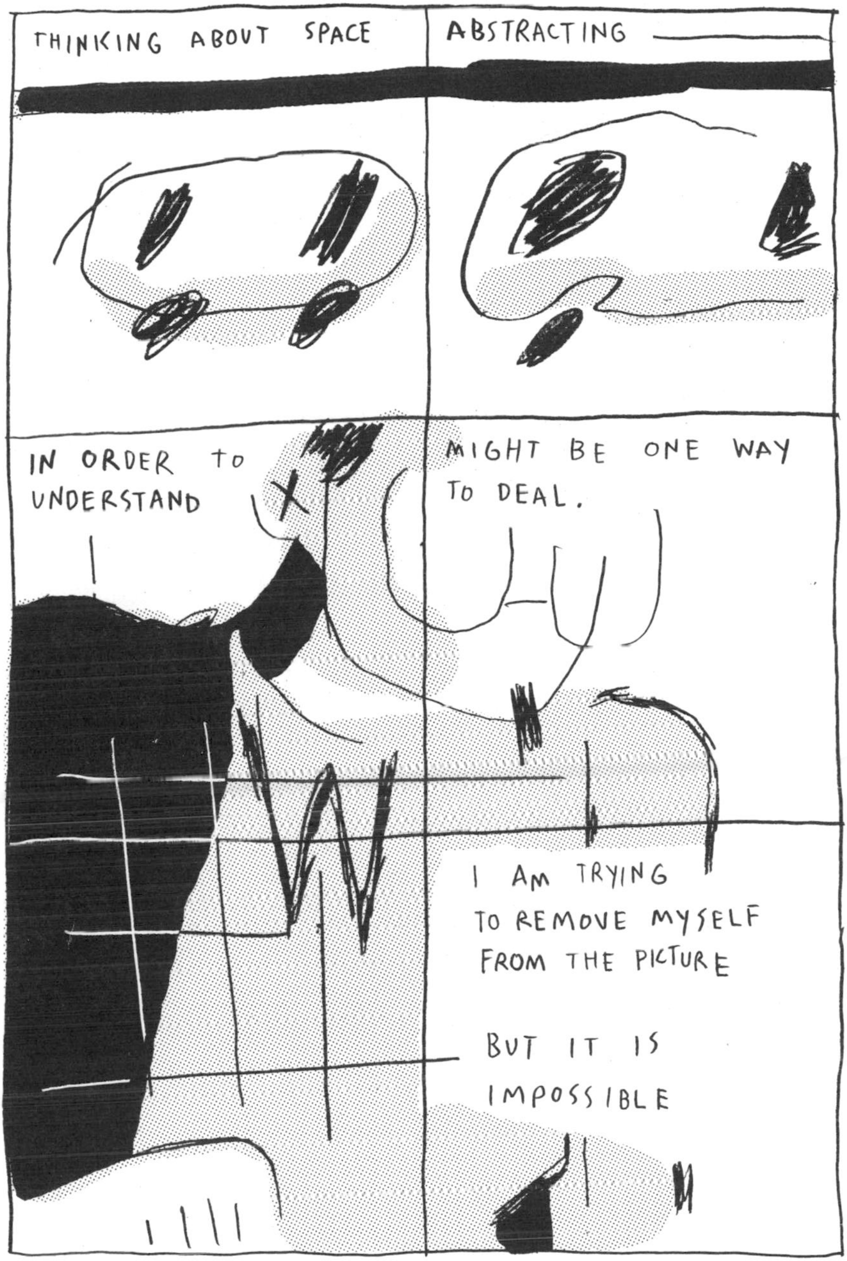
THINKING ABOUT SPACE
ABSTRACTING
IN ORDER TO UNDERSTAND
MIGHT BE ONE WAY TO DEAL.
I AM TRYING TO REMOVE MYSELF FROM THE PICTURE
BUT IT IS IMPOSSIBLE

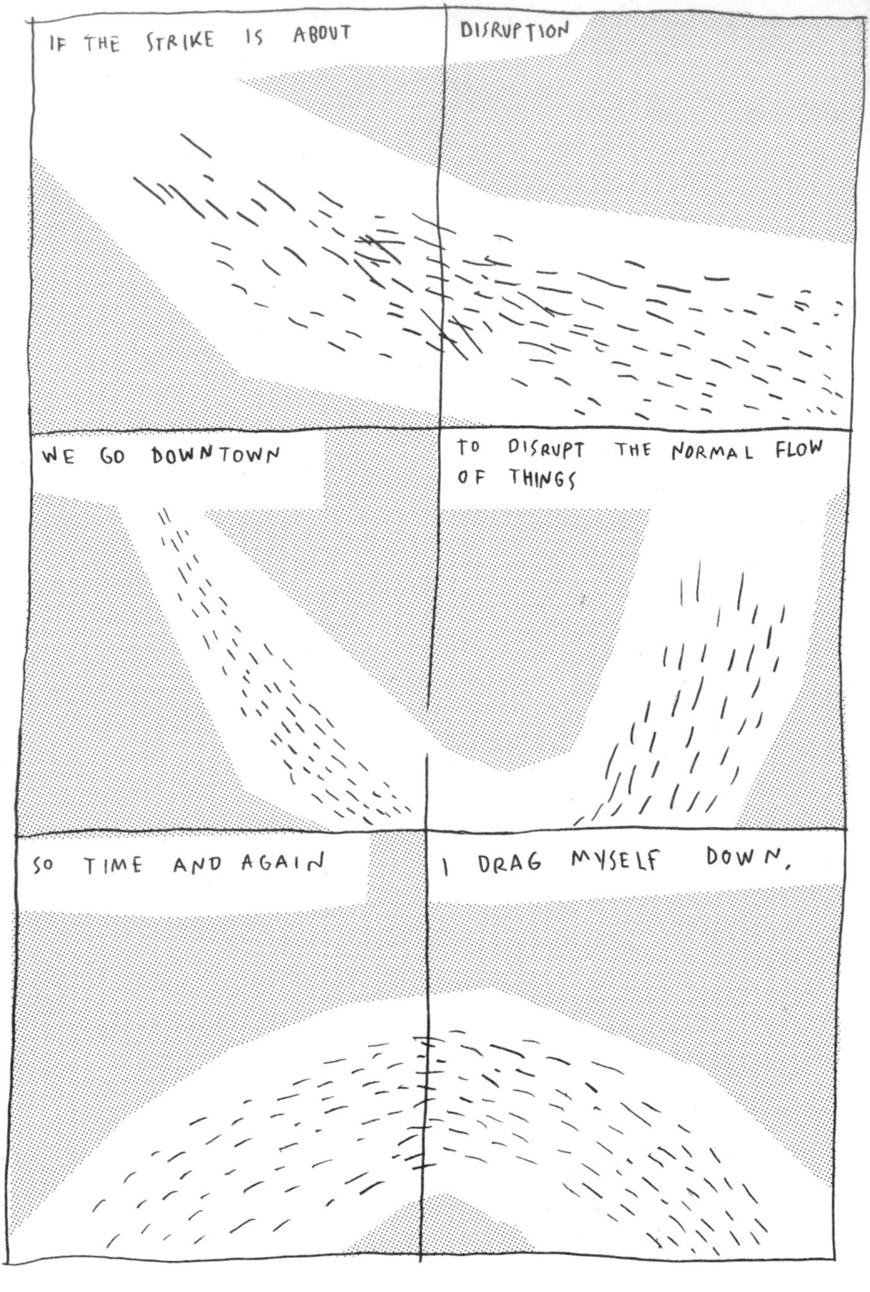
IF THE STRIKE IS ABOUT
DISRUPTION
WE GO DOWNTOWN
TO DISRUPT THE NORMAL FLOW OF THINGS
SO TIME AND AGAIN
I DRAG MYSELF DOWN.

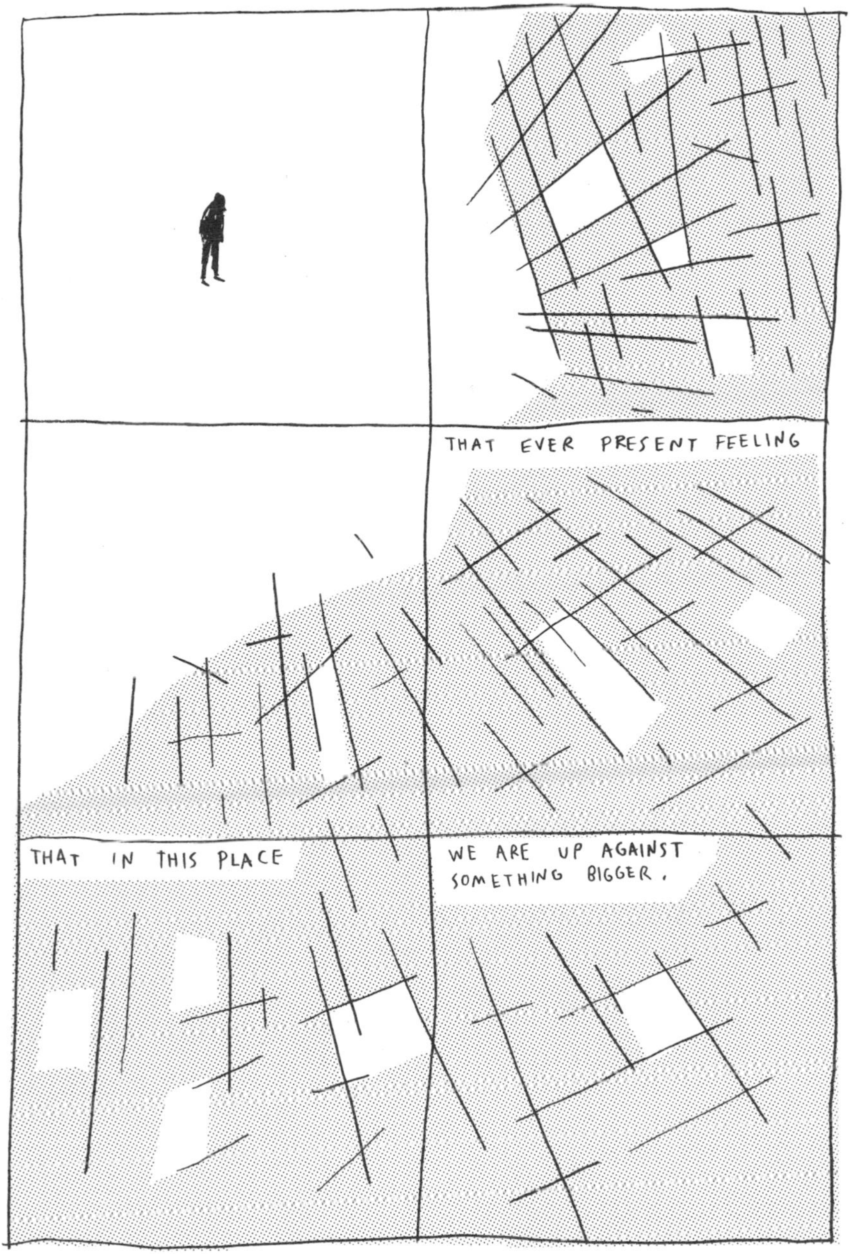
THAT EVER PRESENT FEELING
THAT IN THIS PLACE
WE ARE UP AGAINST SOMETHING BIGGER.

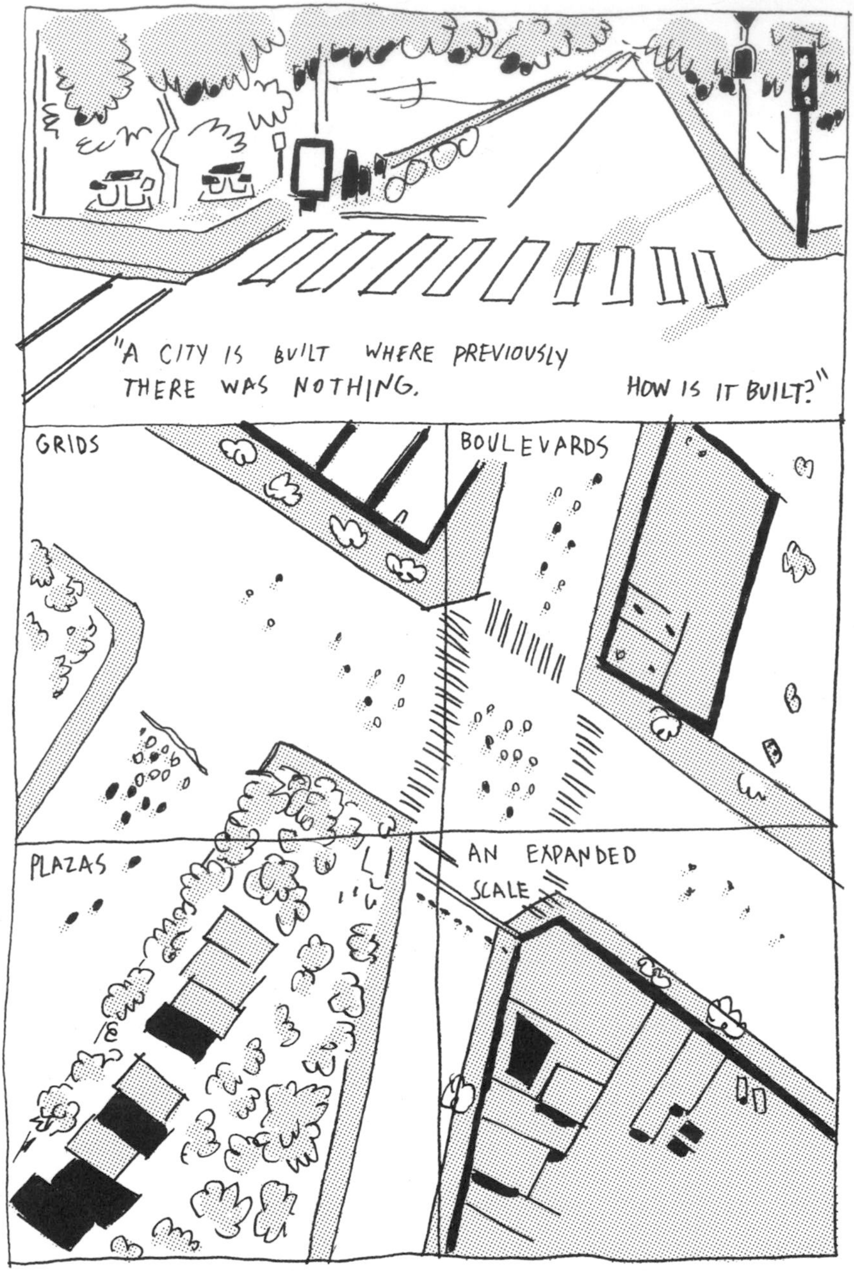
"A CITY IS BUILT WHERE PREVIOUSLY THERE WAS NOTHING.
HOW IS IT BUILT?"
GRIDS
BOULEVARDS
PLAZAS
AN EXPANDED SCALE

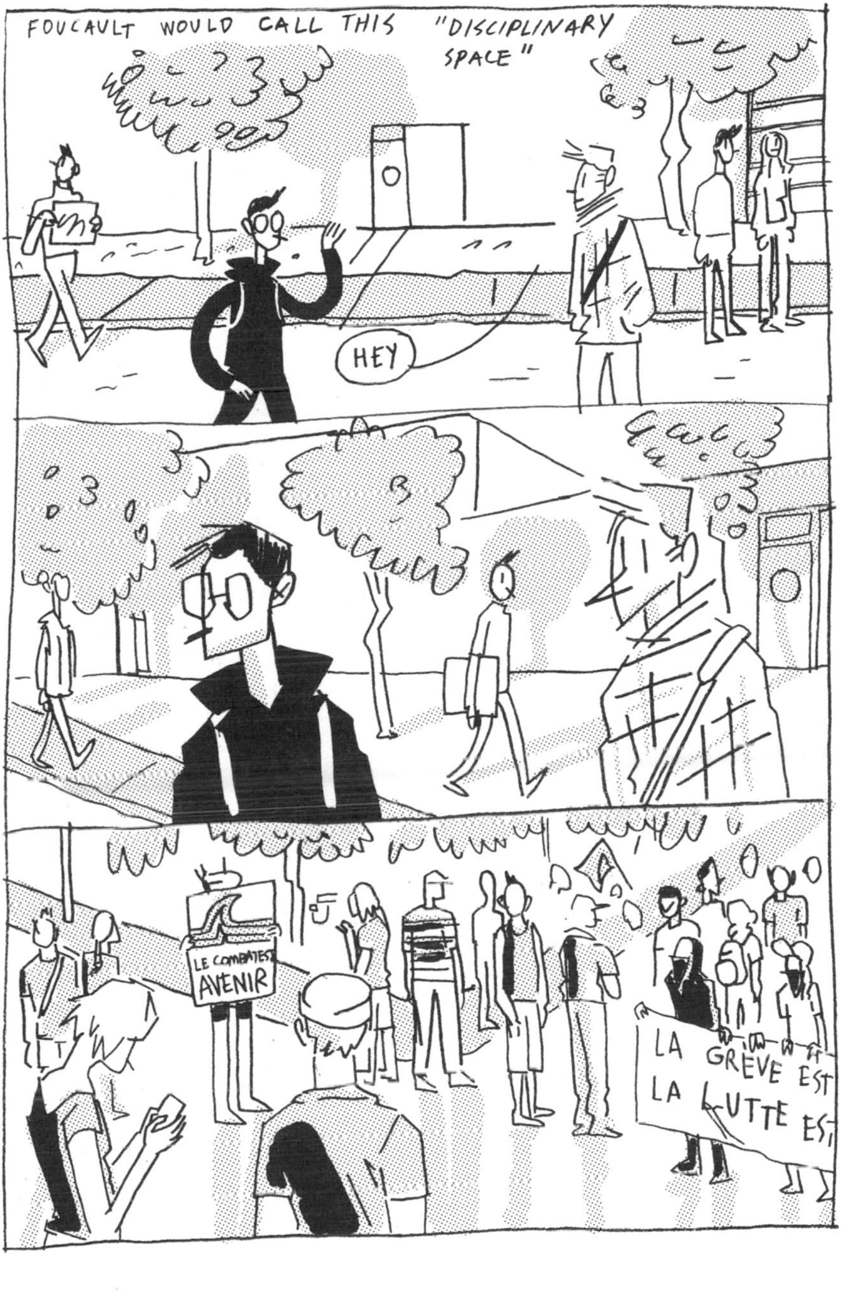
FOUCAULT WOULD CALL THIS "DISCIPLINARY SPACE"
HEY
LE COMBAT EST
AVENIR
LA GREVE EST
LA LUTTE EST

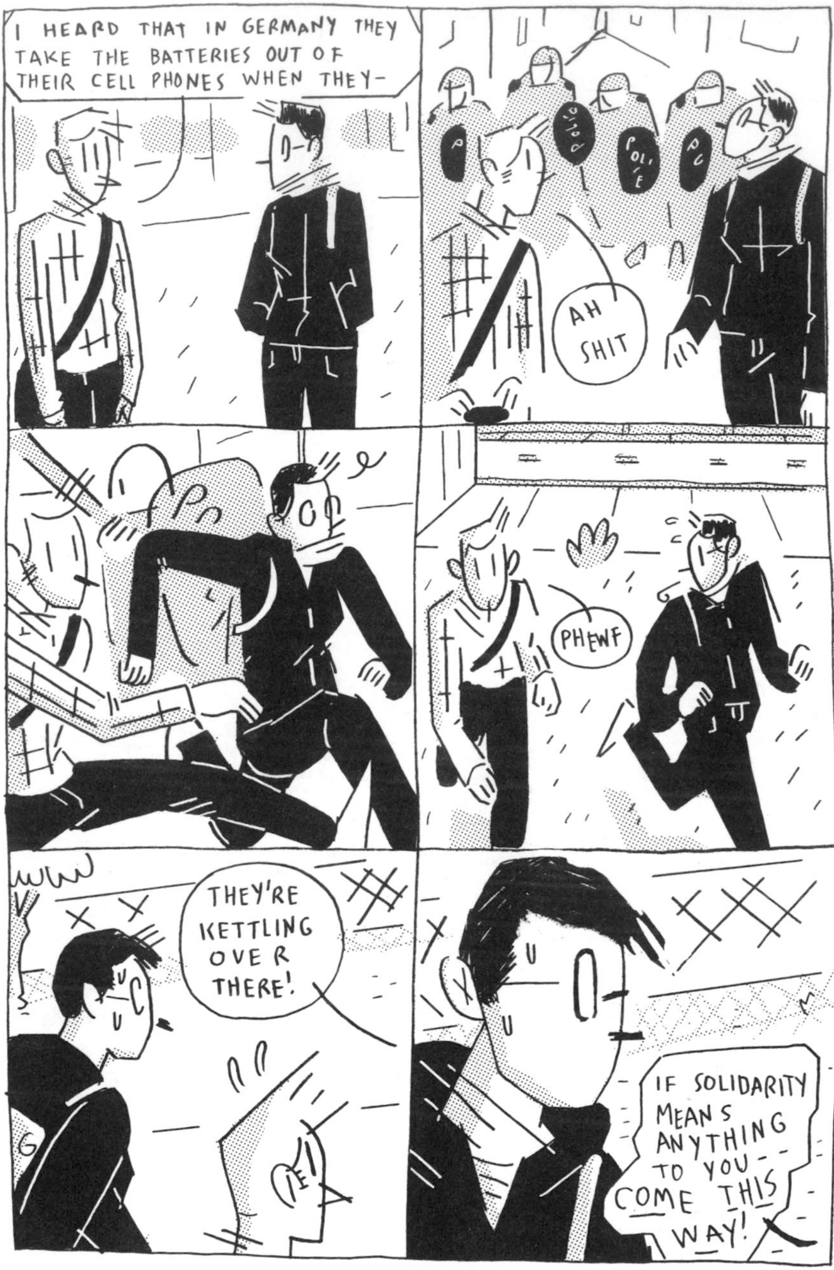
I HEARD THAT IN GERMANY THEY TAKE THE BATTERIES OUT OF THEIR CELL PHONES WHEN THEY-
POLICE
AH SHIT
PHEWF
THEY'RE KETTLING OVER THERE!
IF SOLIDARITY MEANS ANYTHING TO YOU COME THIS WAY!

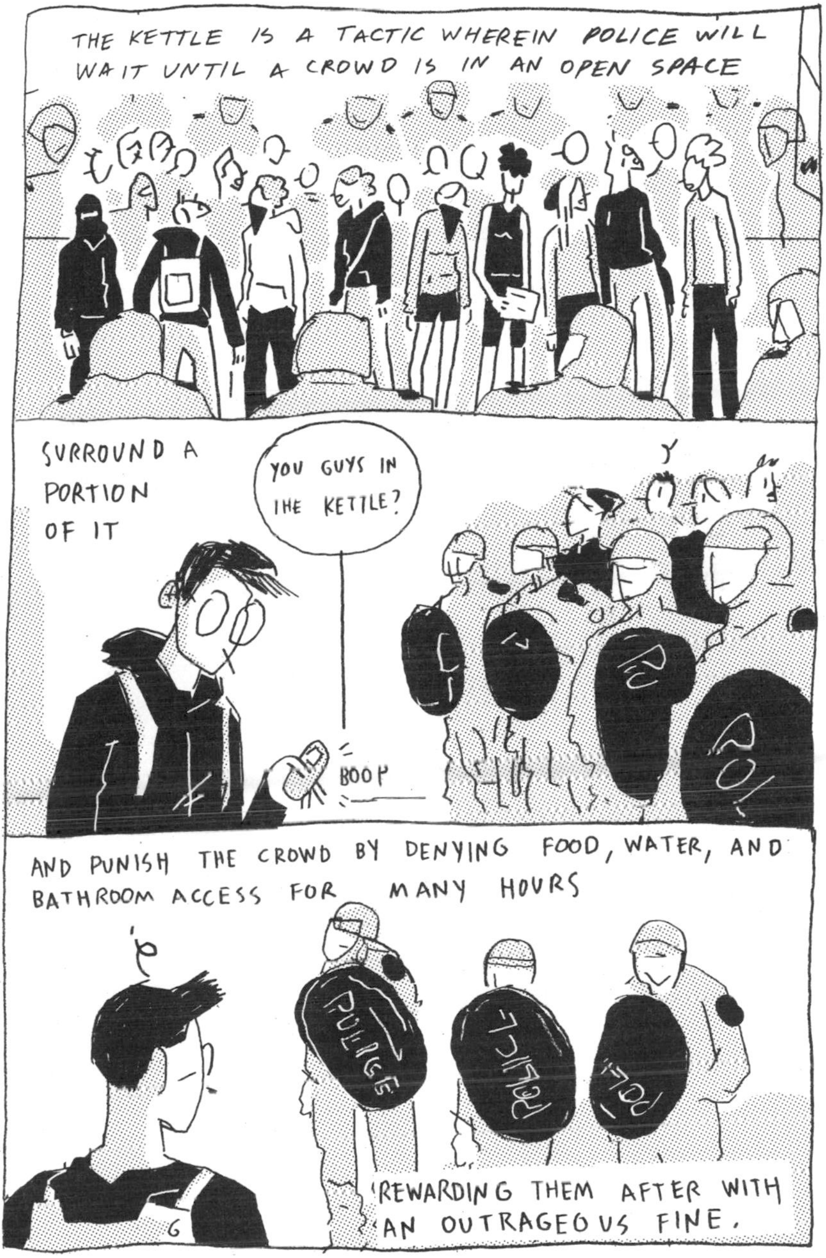
THE KETTLE IS A TACTIC WHEREIN POLICE WILL WAIT UNTIL A CROWD IS IN AN OPEN SPACE
SURROUND A PORTION OF IT
YOU GUYS IN THE KETTLE?
BOOP
AND PUNISH THE CROWD BY DENYING FOOD, WATER, AND BATHROOM ACCESS FOR MANY HOURS
POLICE
REWARDING THEM AFTER WITH AN OUTRAGEOUS FINE.

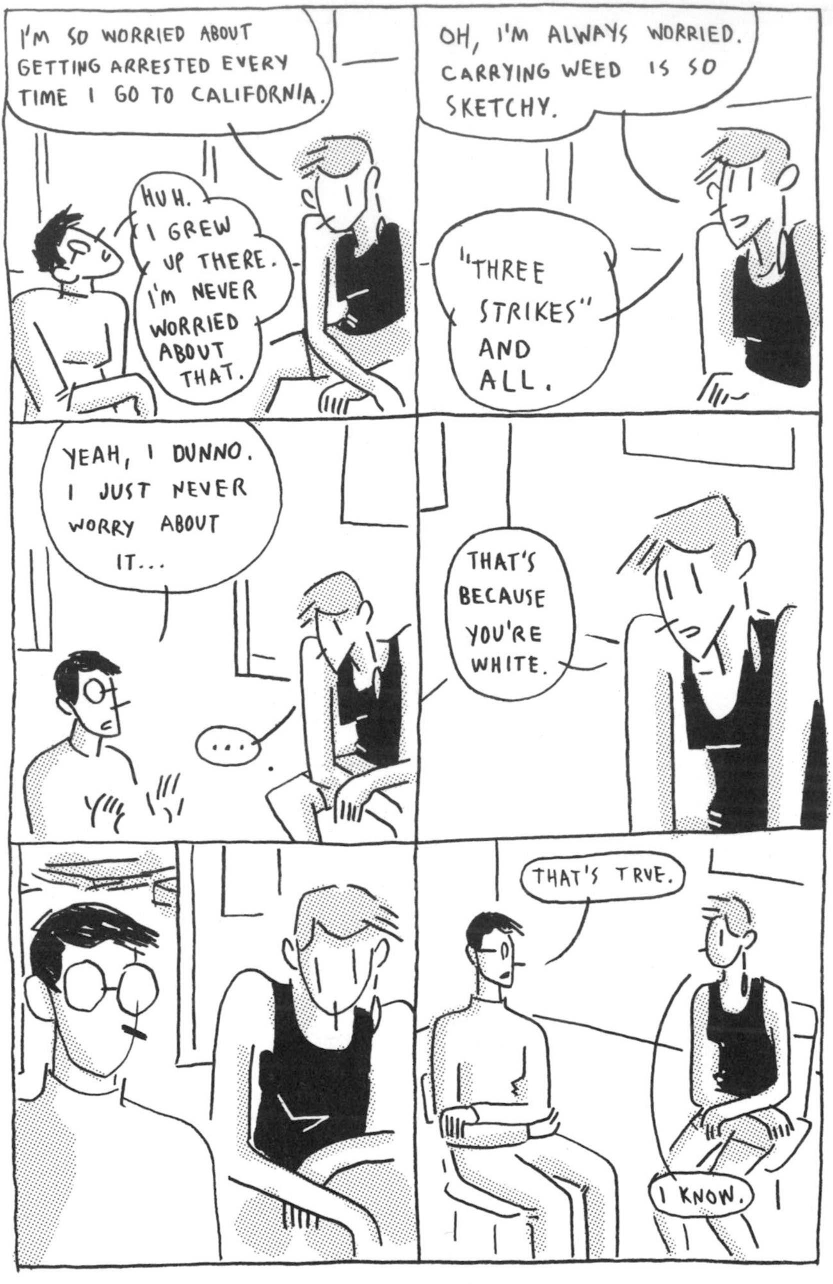
I'M SO WORRIED ABOUT GETTING ARRESTED EVERY TIME I GO TO CALIFORNIA.
HUH. I GREW UP THERE. I'M NEVER WORRIED ABOUT THAT.
OH, I'M ALWAYS WORRIED. CARRYING WEED IS SO SKETCHY.
"THREE STRIKES" AND ALL.
YEAH, I DUNNO. I JUST NEVER WORRY ABOUT IT...
...
THAT'S BECAUSE YOU'RE WHITE.
THAT'S TRUE.
I KNOW.

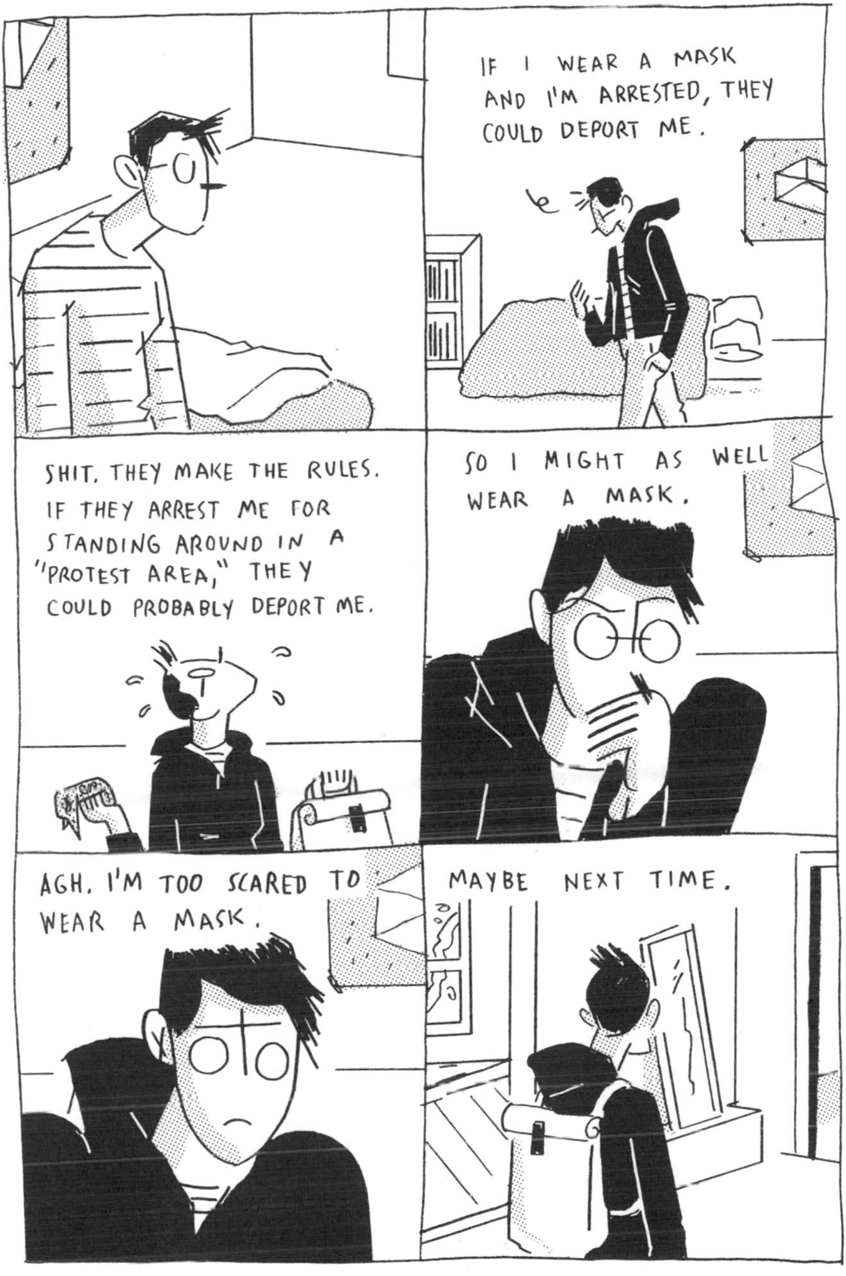
IF I WEAR A MASK AND I'M ARRESTED, THEY COULD DEPORT ME.
SHIT. THEY MAKE THE RULES. IF THEY ARREST ME FOR STANDING AROUND IN A "PROTEST AREA," THEY COULD PROBABLY DEPORT ME.
SO I MIGHT AS WELL WEAR A MASK.
AGH. I'M TOO SCARED TO WEAR A MASK.
MAYBE NEXT TIME.

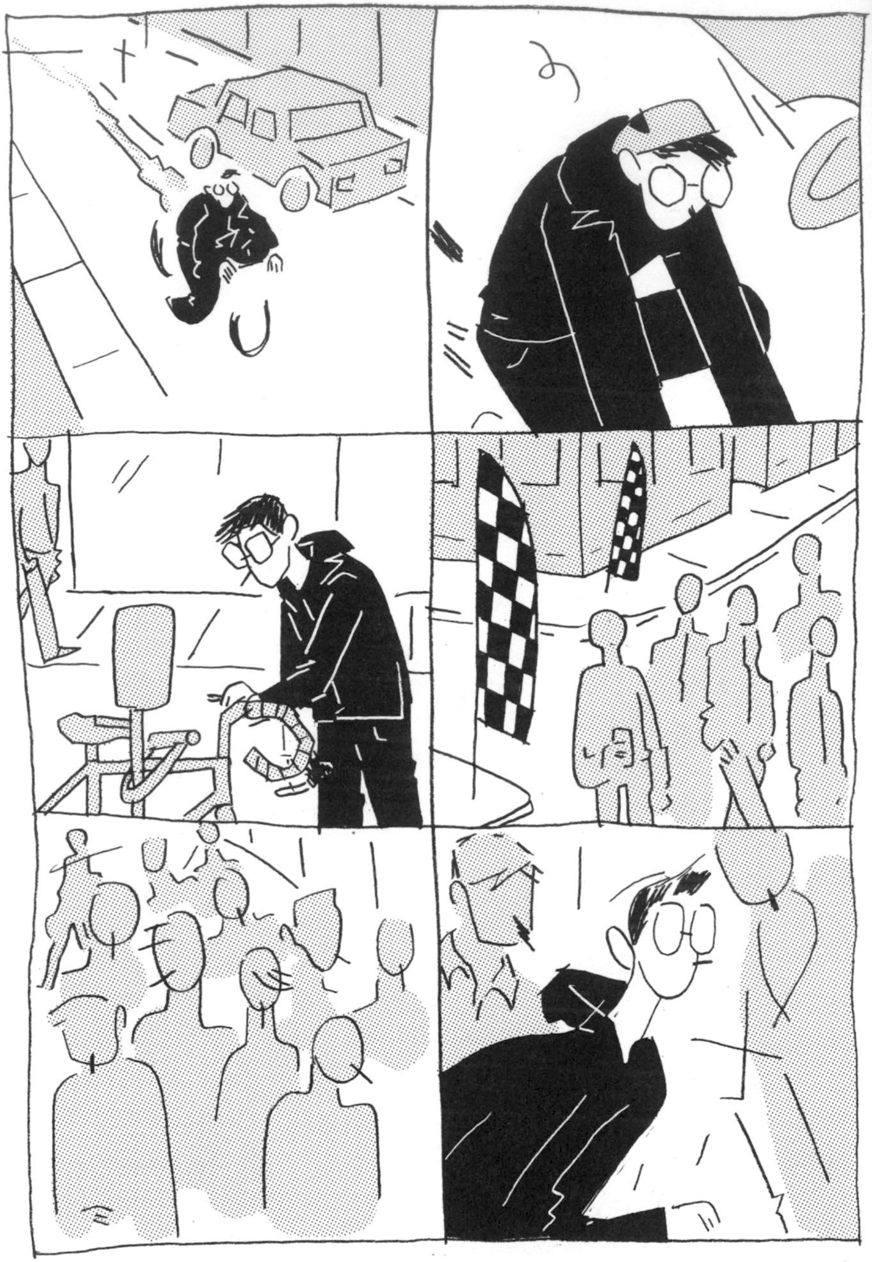

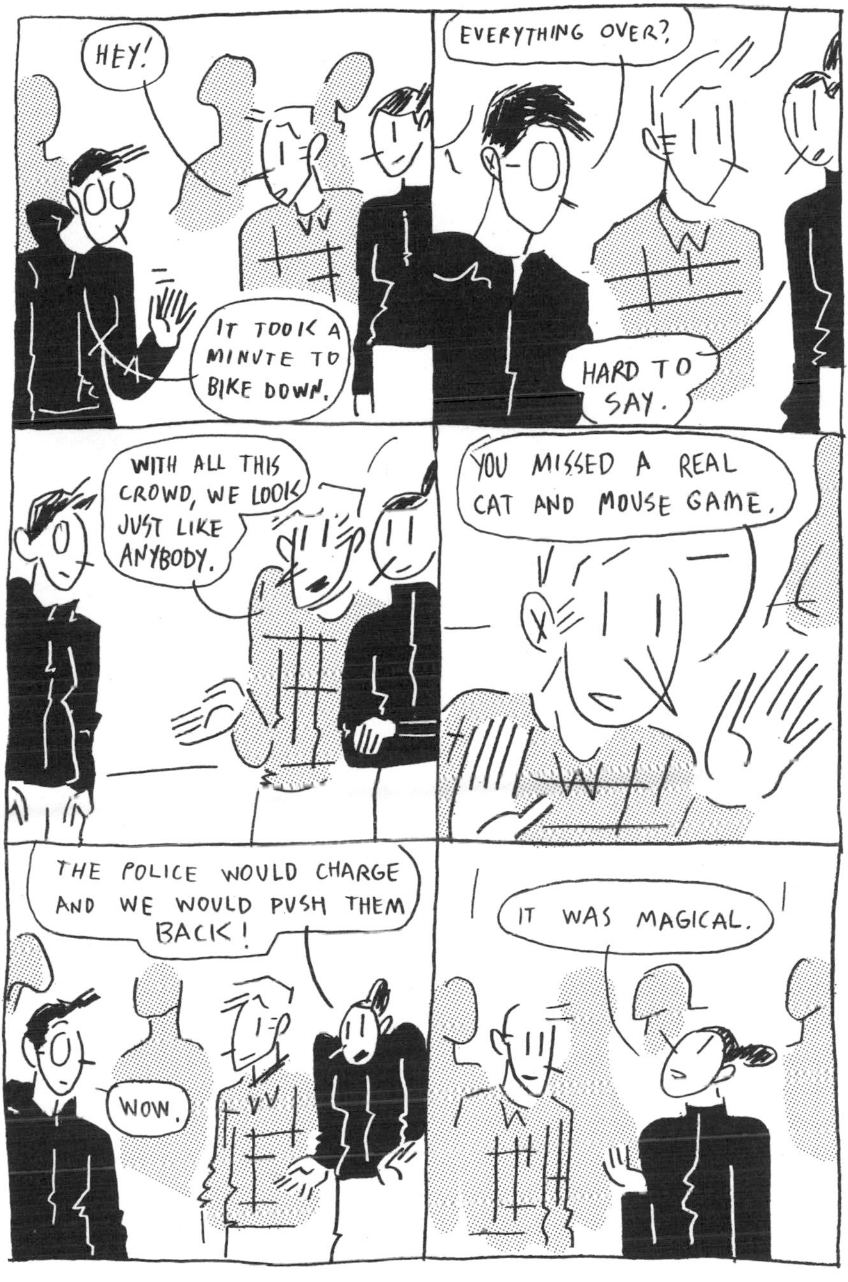
HEY!
IT TOOK A MINUTE TO BIKE DOWN.
EVERYTHING OVER?
HARD TO SAY.
WITH ALL THIS CROWD, WE LOOK JUST LIKE ANYBODY.
YOU MISSED A REAL CAT AND MOUSE GAME.
THE POLICE WOULD CHARGE AND WE WOULD PUSH THEM BACK!
WOW.
IT WAS MAGICAL.

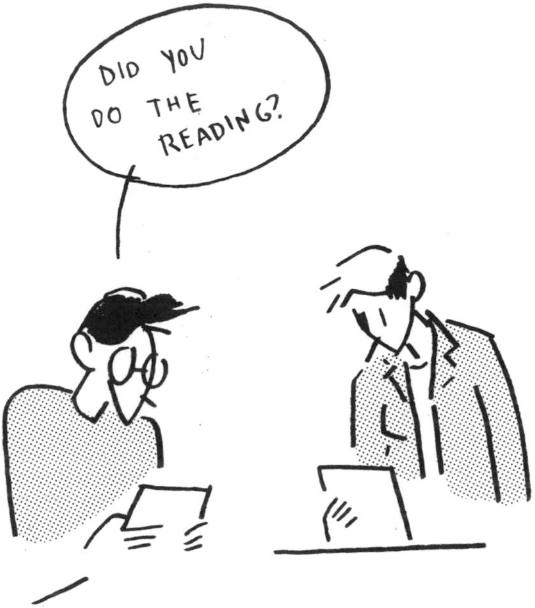
DID YOU DO THE READING?

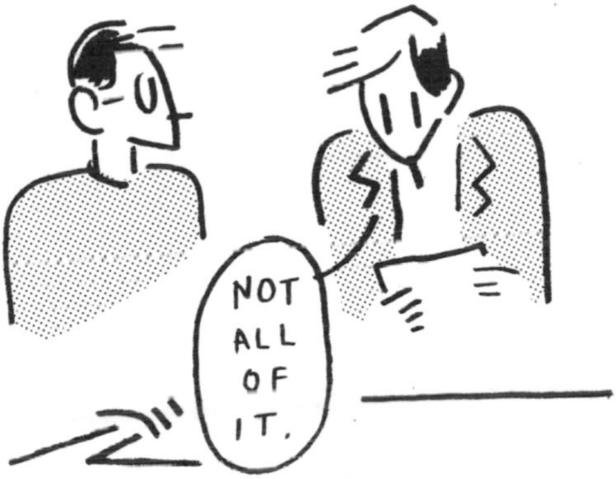
NOT ALL OF IT.

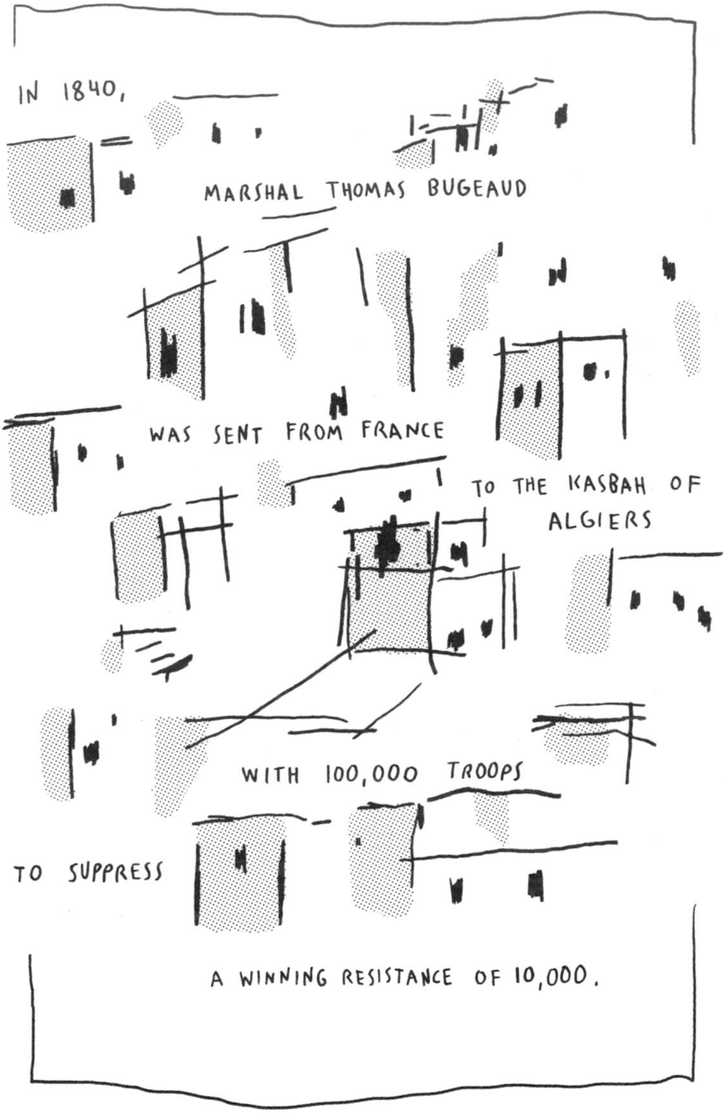
IN 1840,
MARSHAL THOMAS BUGEAUD
WAS SENT FROM FRANCE
TO THE KASBAH OF ALGIERS
WITH 100,000 TROOPS
TO SUPPRESS
A WINNING RESISTANCE OF 10,000.

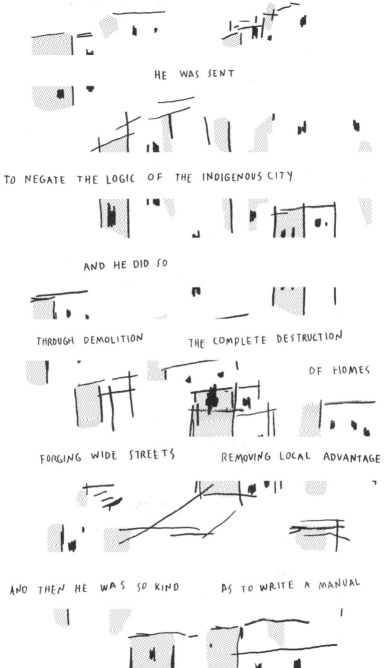

HE WAS SENT

TO NEGATE THE LOGIC OF THE INDIGENOUS CITY

AND HE DID SO

THROUGH DEMOLITION   THE COMPLETE DESTRUCTION

OF HOMES

FORGING WIDE STREETS   REMOVING LOCAL ADVANTAGE

AND THEN HE WAS SO KIND   AS TO WRITE A MANUAL

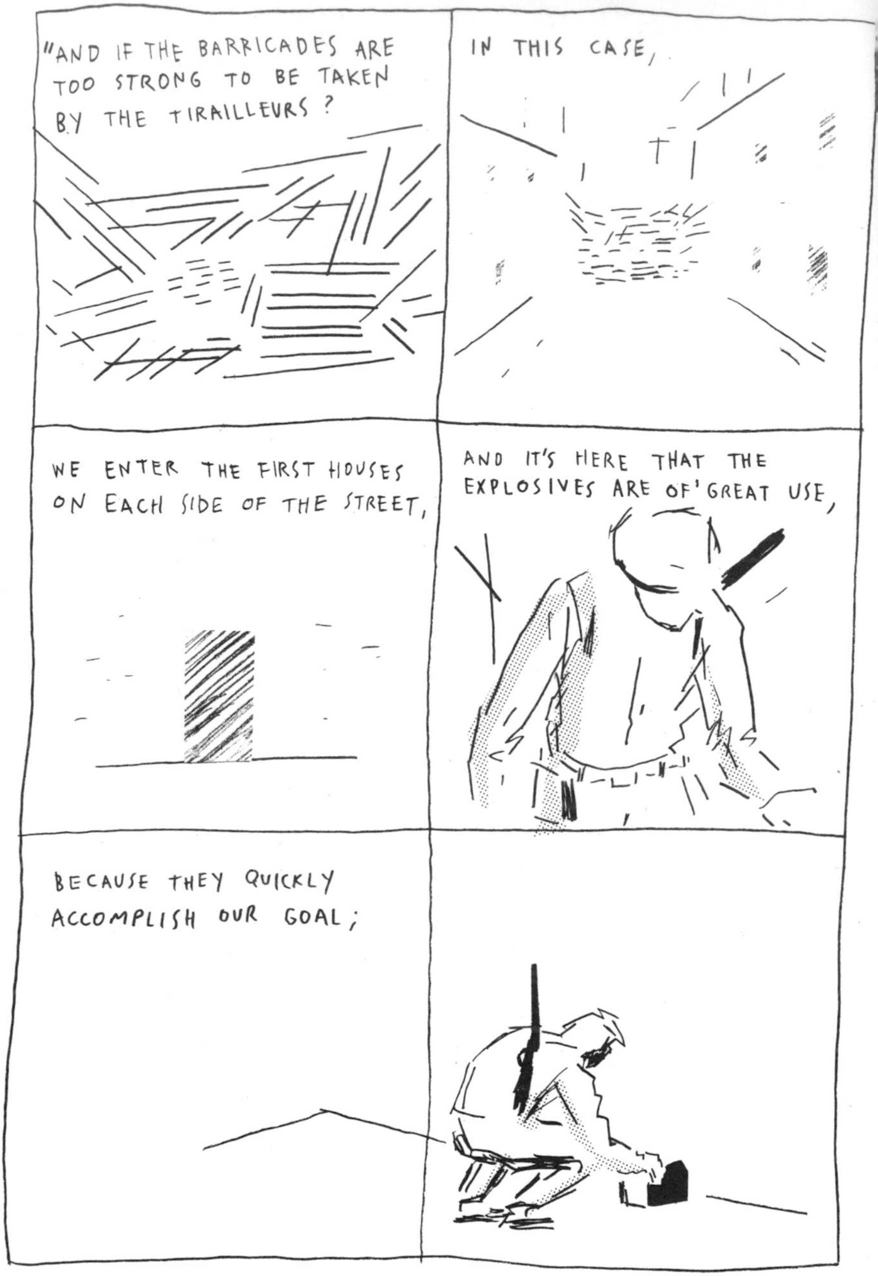

"AND IF THE BARRICADES ARE TOO STRONG TO BE TAKEN BY THE TIRAILLEURS ?
IN THIS CASE,
WE ENTER THE FIRST HOUSES ON EACH SIDE OF THE STREET,
AND IT'S HERE THAT THE EXPLOSIVES ARE OF GREAT USE,
BECAUSE THEY QUICKLY ACCOMPLISH OUR GOAL;

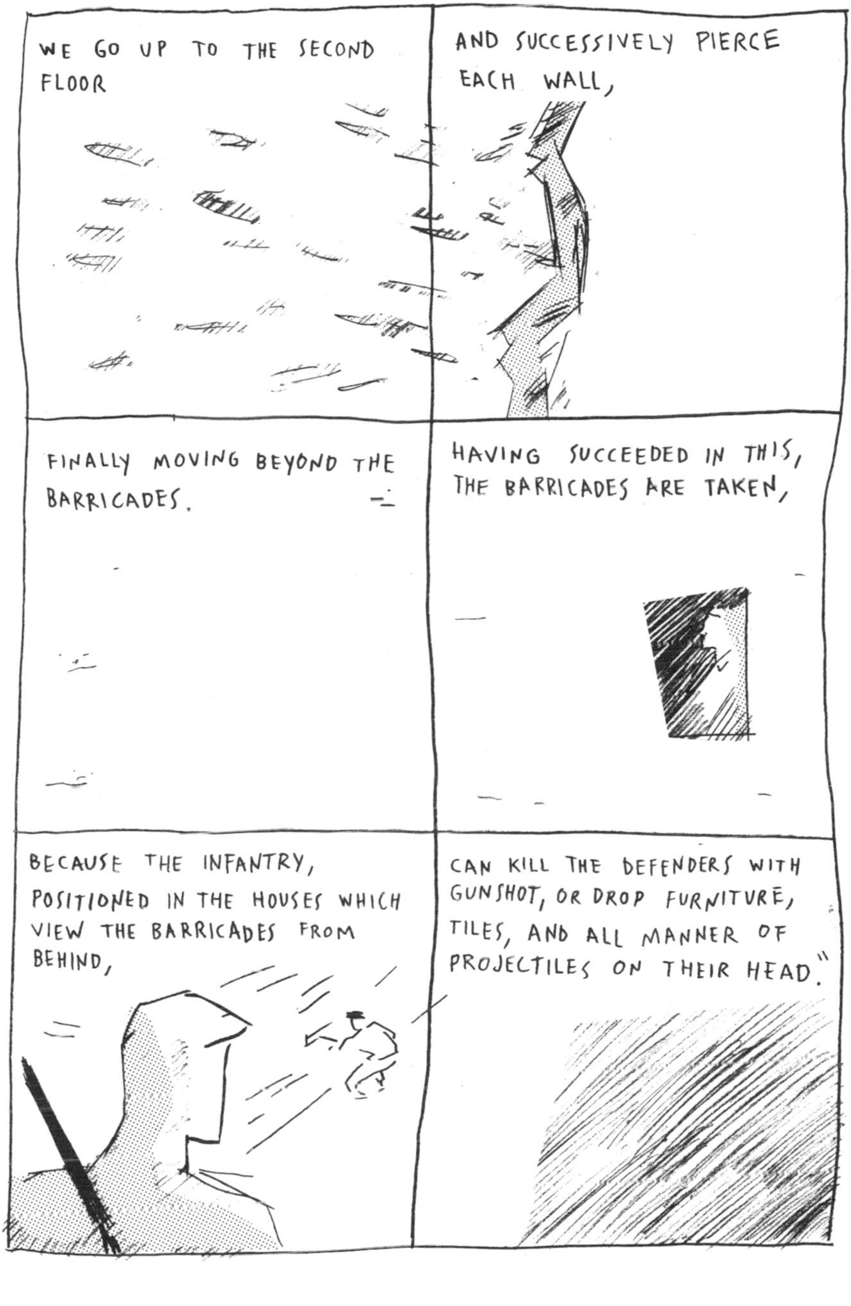
WE GO UP TO THE SECOND FLOOR
AND SUCCESSIVELY PIERCE EACH WALL,
FINALLY MOVING BEYOND THE BARRICADES.
HAVING SUCCEEDED IN THIS, THE BARRICADES ARE TAKEN,
BECAUSE THE INFANTRY, POSITIONED IN THE HOUSES WHICH VIEW THE BARRICADES FROM BEHIND,
CAN KILL THE DEFENDERS WITH GUNSHOT, OR DROP FURNITURE, TILES, AND ALL MANNER OF PROJECTILES ON THEIR HEAD."

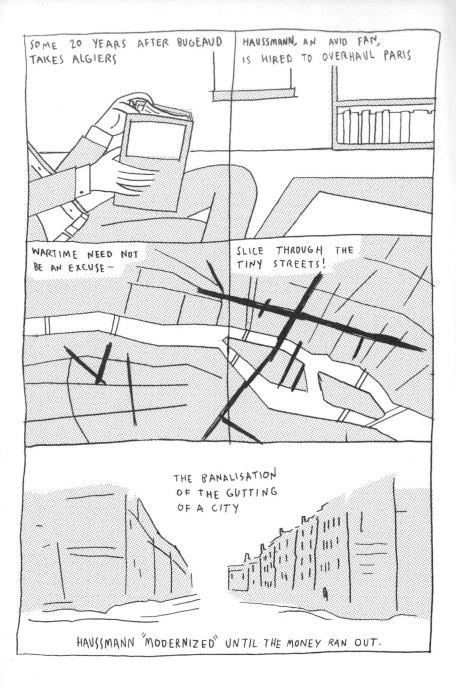

SOME 20 YEARS AFTER BUGEAUD TAKES ALGIERS

HAUSSMANN, AN AVID FAN, IS HIRED TO OVERHAUL PARIS

WARTIME NEED NOT BE AN EXCUSE —

SLICE THROUGH THE TINY STREETS!

THE BANALISATION OF THE GUTTING OF A CITY

HAUSSMANN "MODERNIZED" UNTIL THE MONEY RAN OUT.

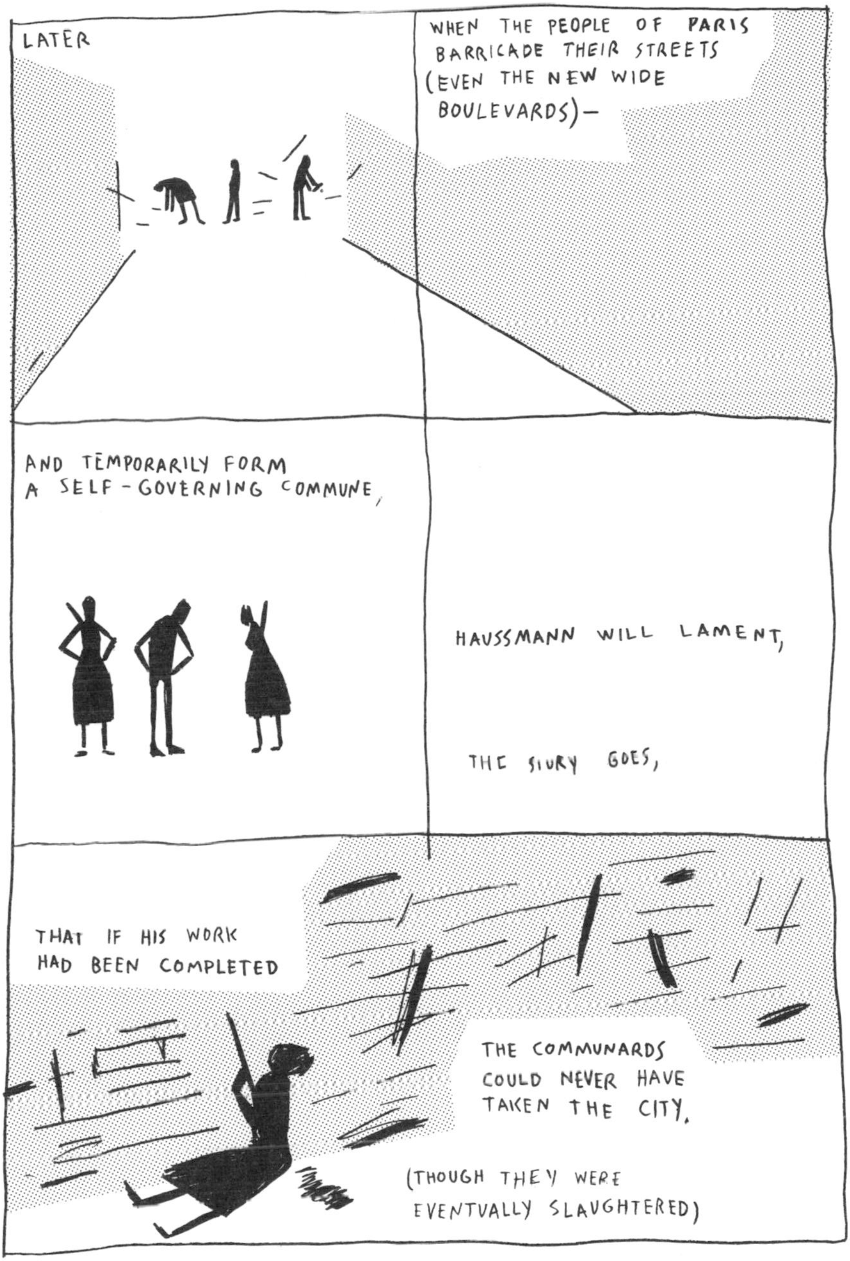
LATER
WHEN THE PEOPLE OF PARIS BARRICADE THEIR STREETS (EVEN THE NEW WIDE BOULEVARDS)—
AND TEMPORARILY FORM A SELF-GOVERNING COMMUNE,
HAUSSMANN WILL LAMENT,
THE STORY GOES,
THAT IF HIS WORK HAD BEEN COMPLETED
THE COMMUNARDS COULD NEVER HAVE TAKEN THE CITY.
(THOUGH THEY WERE EVENTUALLY SLAUGHTERED)

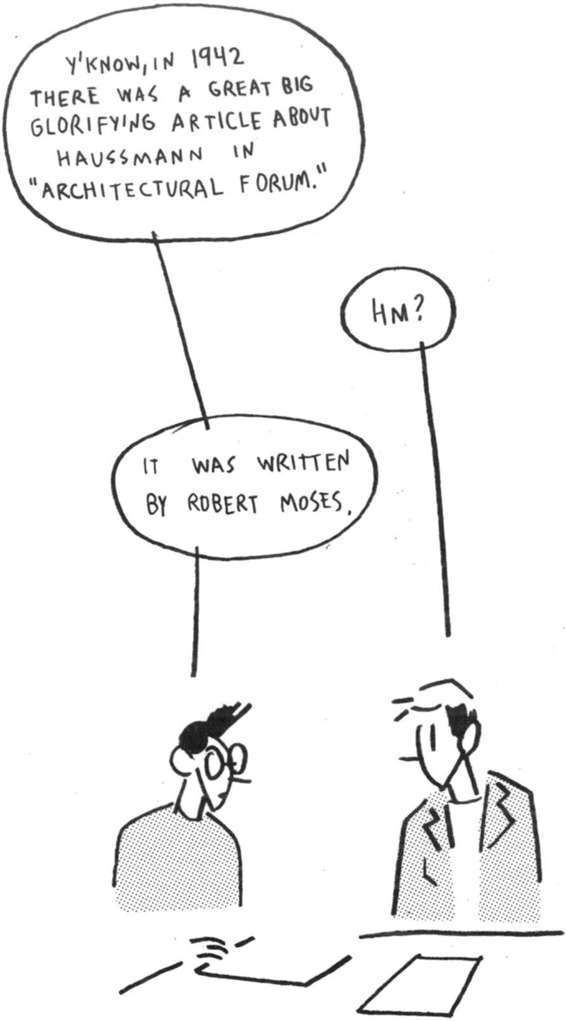
Y'KNOW, IN 1942 THERE WAS A GREAT BIG GLORIFYING ARTICLE ABOUT HAUSSMANN IN "ARCHITECTURAL FORUM."
HM?
IT WAS WRITTEN BY ROBERT MOSES.

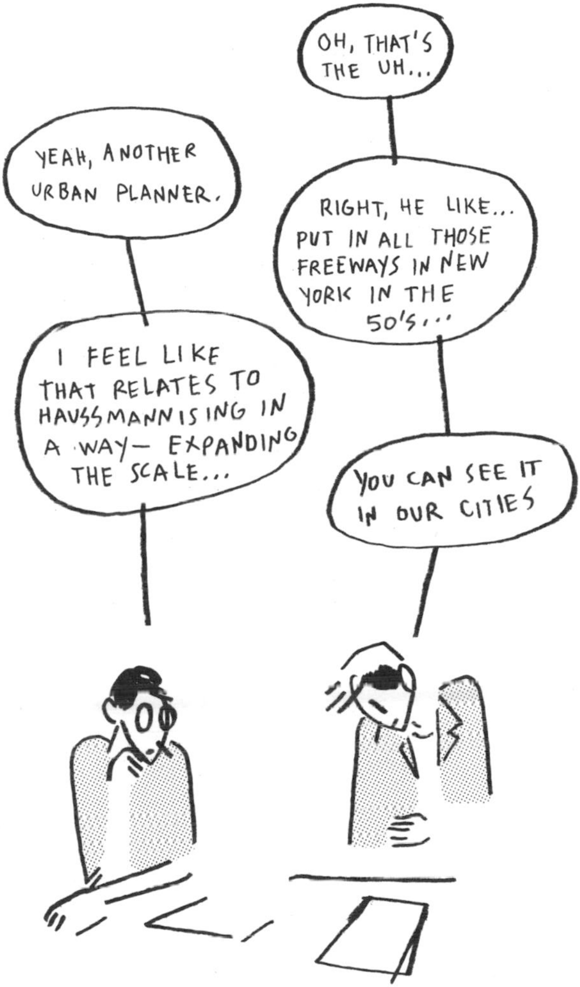
OH, THAT'S THE UH...
YEAH, ANOTHER URBAN PLANNER.
RIGHT, HE LIKE... PUT IN ALL THOSE FREEWAYS IN NEW YORK IN THE 50'S...
I FEEL LIKE THAT RELATES TO HAUSSMANNISING IN A WAY— EXPANDING THE SCALE...
YOU CAN SEE IT IN OUR CITIES

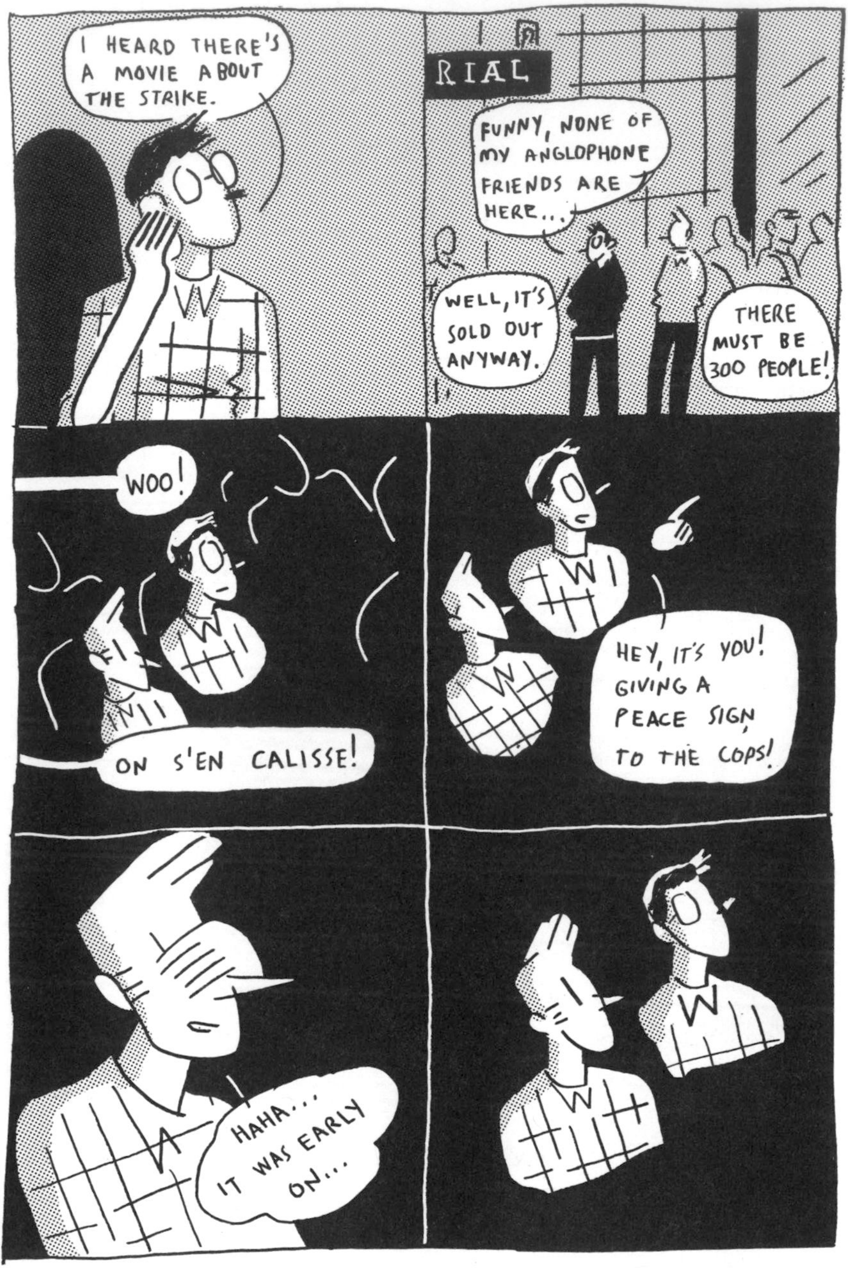
I HEARD THERE'S A MOVIE ABOUT THE STRIKE.
RIAL
FUNNY, NONE OF MY ANGLOPHONE FRIENDS ARE HERE...
WELL, IT'S SOLD OUT ANYWAY.
THERE MUST BE 300 PEOPLE!
WOO!
ON S'EN CALISSE!
HEY, IT'S YOU! GIVING A PEACE SIGN, TO THE COPS!
HAHA... IT WAS EARLY ON...

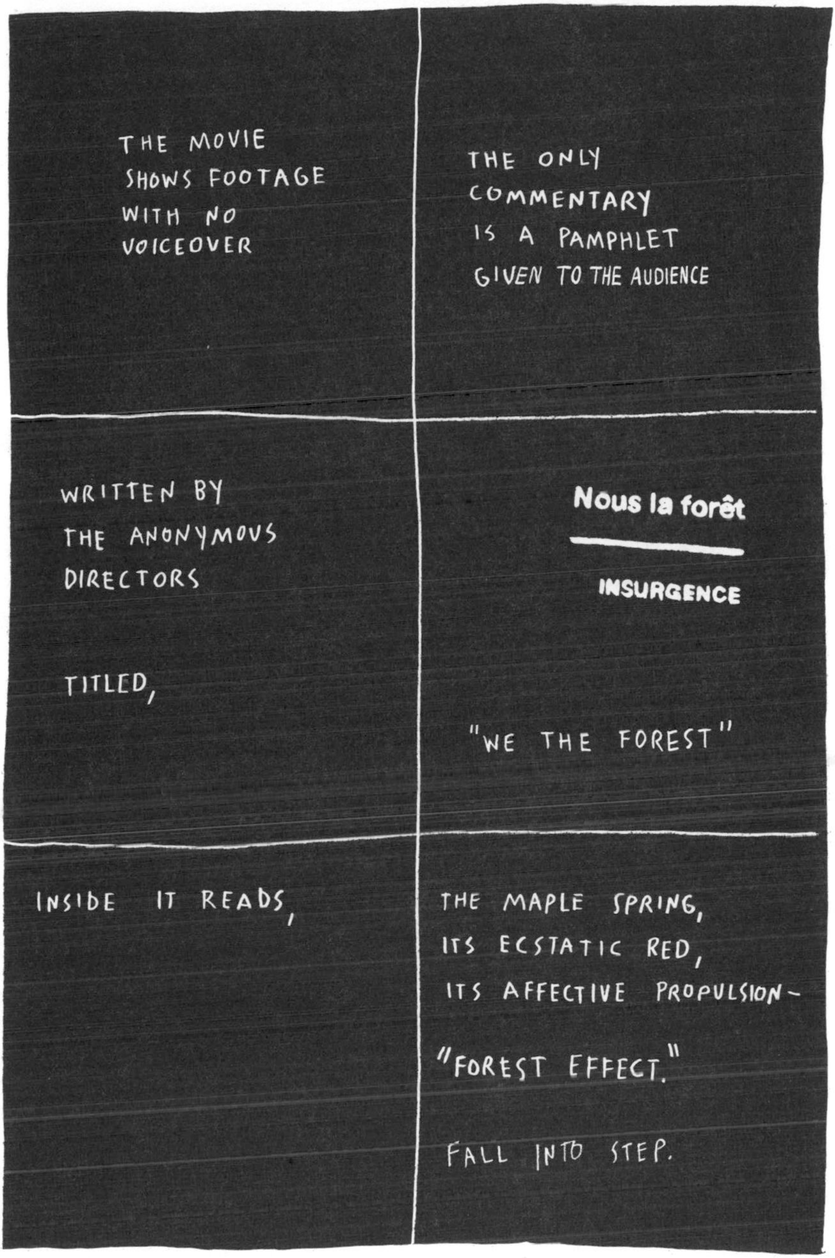
THE MOVIE SHOWS FOOTAGE WITH NO VOICEOVER
THE ONLY COMMENTARY IS A PAMPHLET GIVEN TO THE AUDIENCE
WRITTEN BY THE ANONYMOUS DIRECTORS
TITLED,
Nous la forêt
INSURGENCE
"WE THE FOREST"
INSIDE IT READS,
THE MAPLE SPRING, ITS ECSTATIC RED, ITS AFFECTIVE PROPULSION-
"FOREST EFFECT."
FALL INTO STEP.

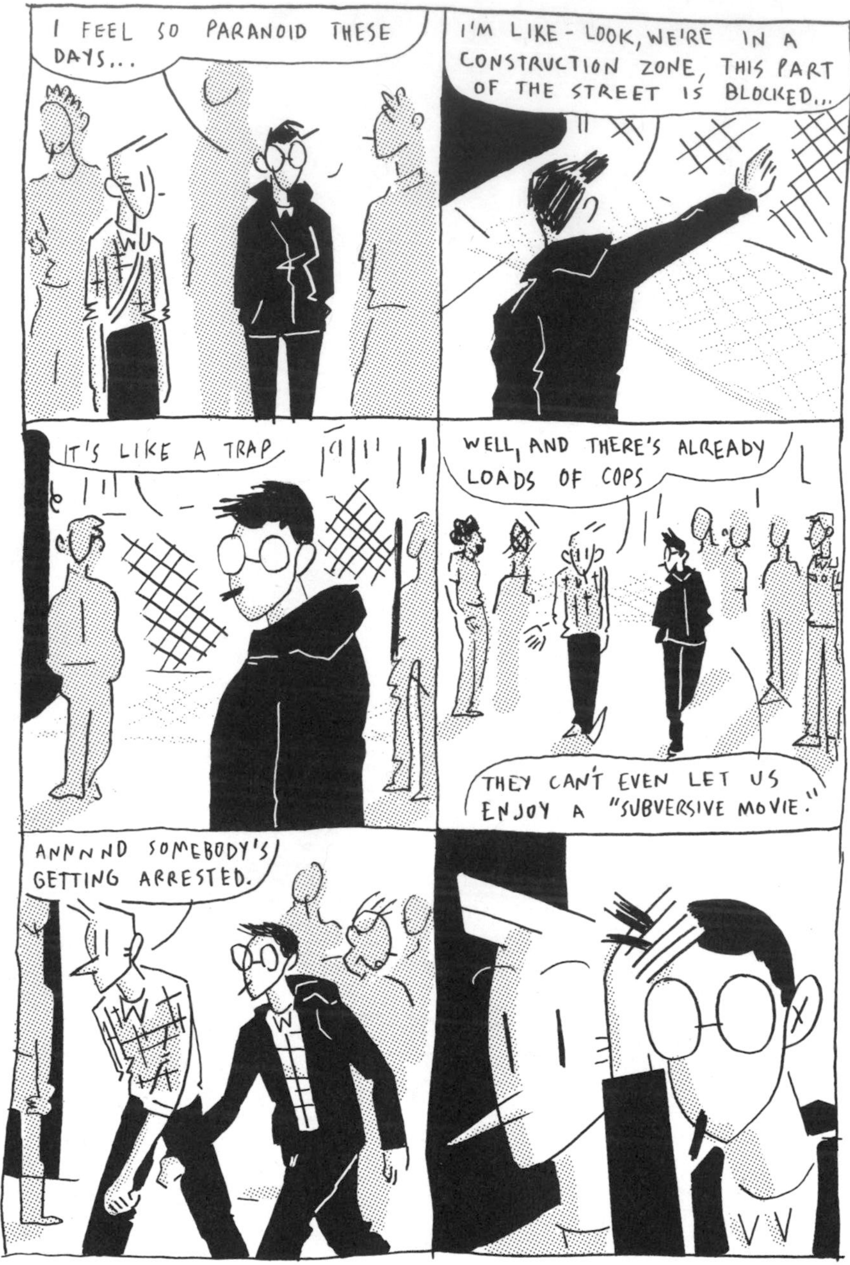
I FEEL SO PARANOID THESE DAYS...
I'M LIKE - LOOK, WE'RE IN A CONSTRUCTION ZONE, THIS PART OF THE STREET IS BLOCKED...
IT'S LIKE A TRAP
WELL, AND THERE'S ALREADY LOADS OF COPS
THEY CAN'T EVEN LET US ENJOY A "SUBVERSIVE MOVIE."
ANNNND SOMEBODY'S GETTING ARRESTED.

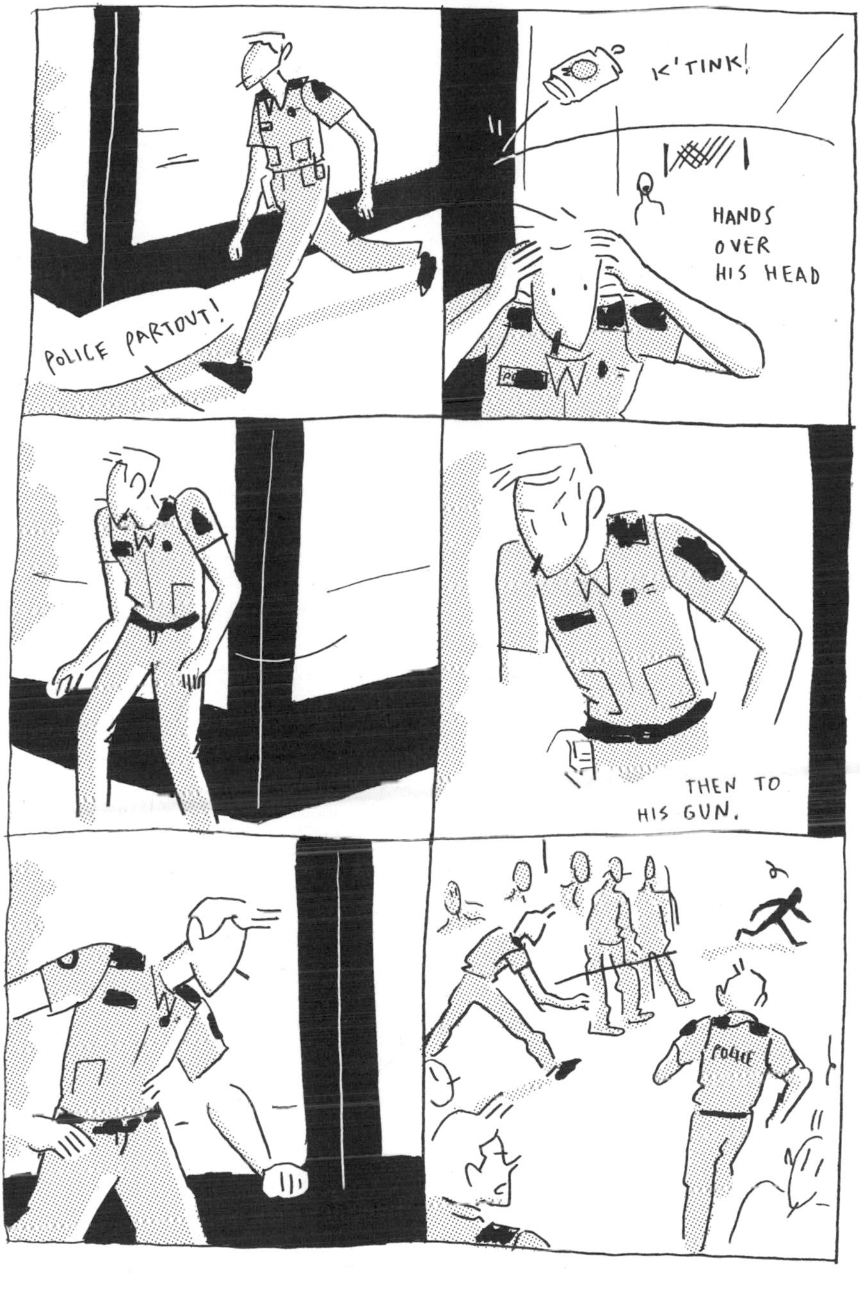
POLICE PARTOUT!
K'TINK!
HANDS OVER HIS HEAD
THEN TO HIS GUN.
POLICE

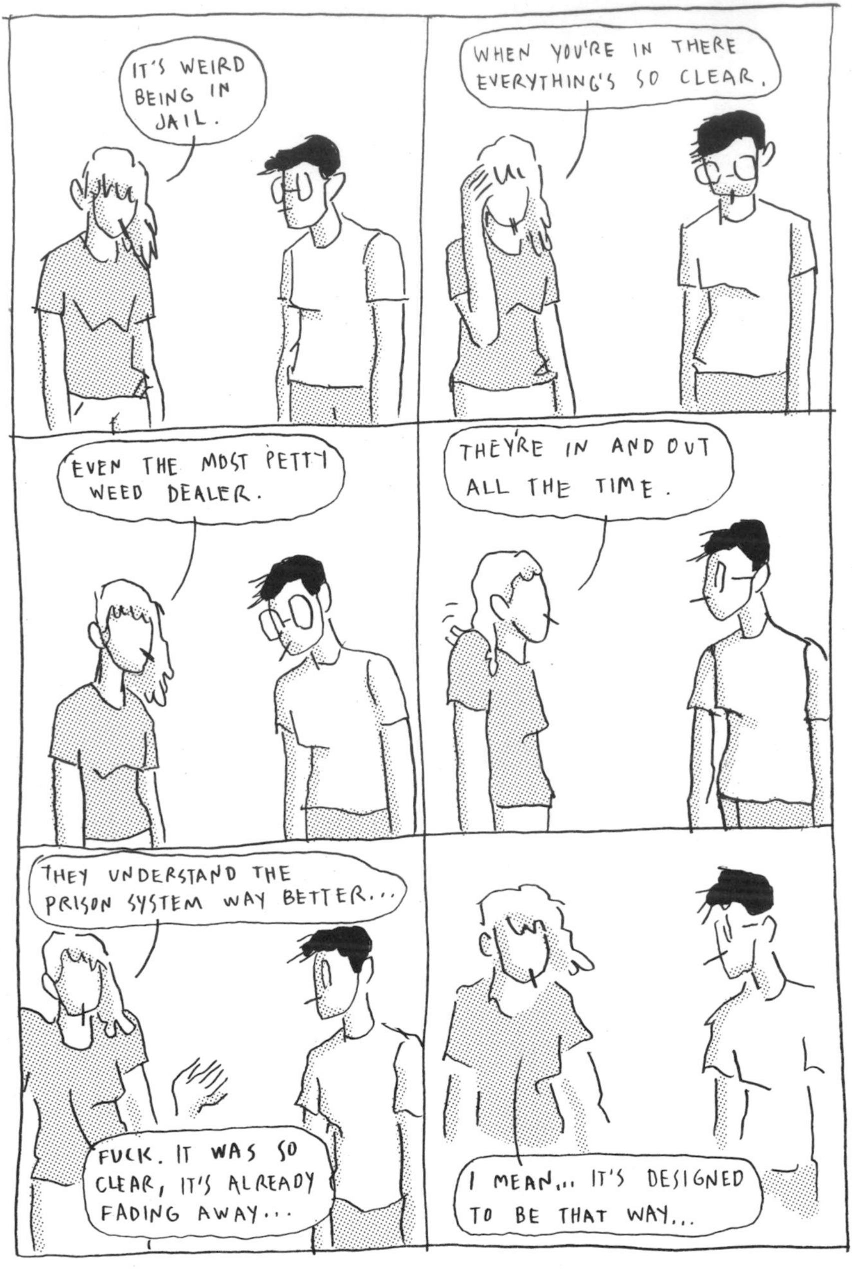
IT'S WEIRD BEING IN JAIL.
WHEN YOU'RE IN THERE EVERYTHING'S SO CLEAR.
EVEN THE MOST PETTY WEED DEALER.
THEY'RE IN AND OUT ALL THE TIME.
THEY UNDERSTAND THE PRISON SYSTEM WAY BETTER...
FUCK. IT WAS SO CLEAR, IT'S ALREADY FADING AWAY...
I MEAN... IT'S DESIGNED TO BE THAT WAY...

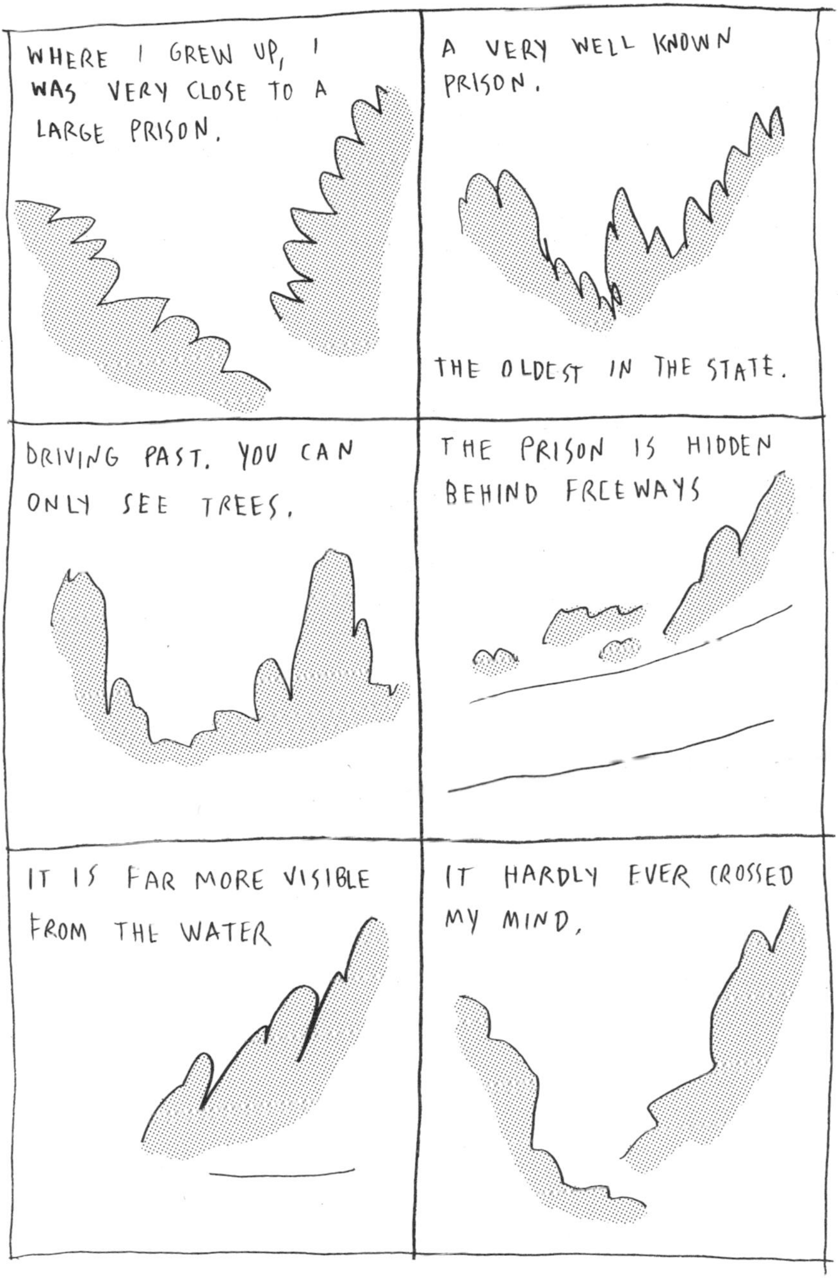
WHERE I GREW UP, I WAS VERY CLOSE TO A LARGE PRISON.
A VERY WELL KNOWN PRISON.
THE OLDEST IN THE STATE.
DRIVING PAST. YOU CAN ONLY SEE TREES.
THE PRISON IS HIDDEN BEHIND FREEWAYS
IT IS FAR MORE VISIBLE FROM THE WATER
IT HARDLY EVER CROSSED MY MIND.

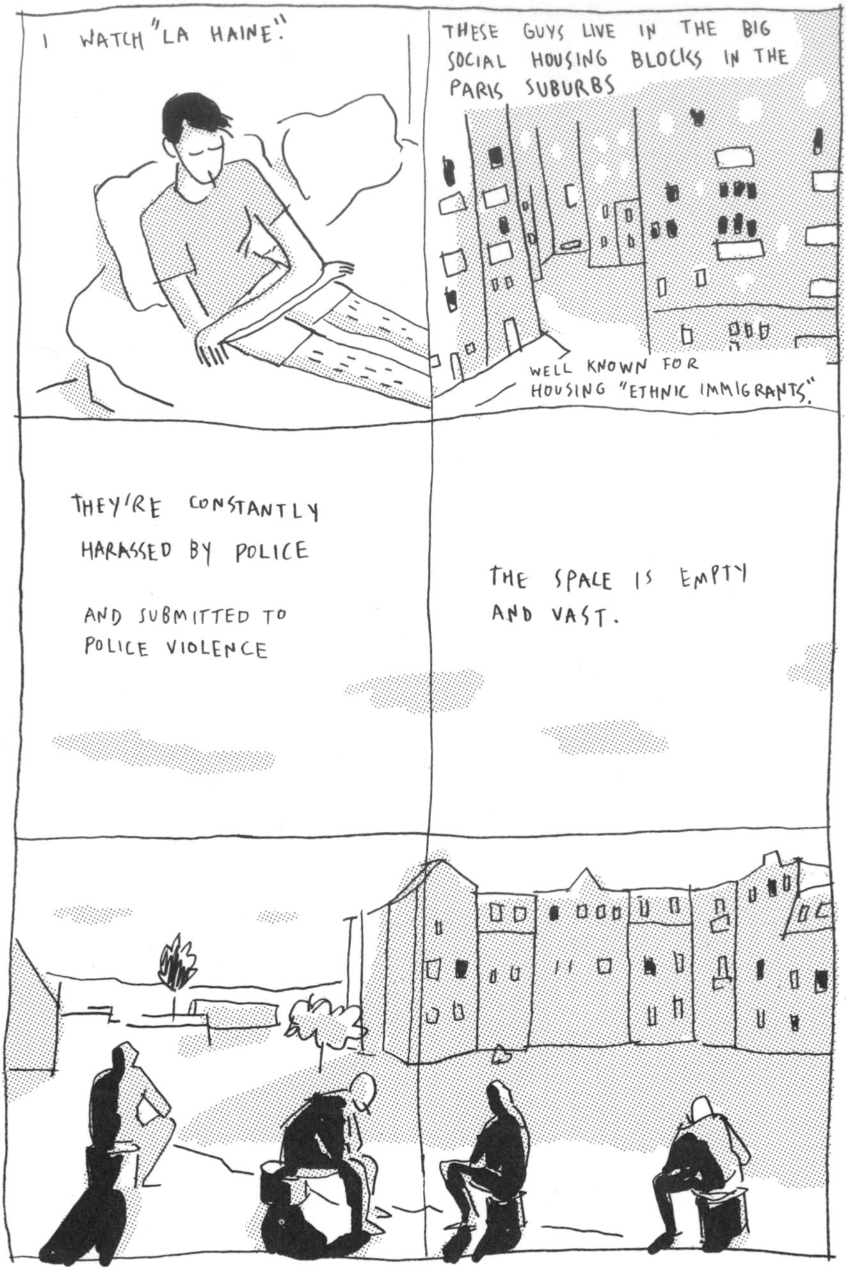
I WATCH "LA HAINE."
THESE GUYS LIVE IN THE BIG SOCIAL HOUSING BLOCKS IN THE PARIS SUBURBS
WELL KNOWN FOR HOUSING "ETHNIC IMMIGRANTS."
THEY'RE CONSTANTLY HARASSED BY POLICE
AND SUBMITTED TO POLICE VIOLENCE
THE SPACE IS EMPTY AND VAST.

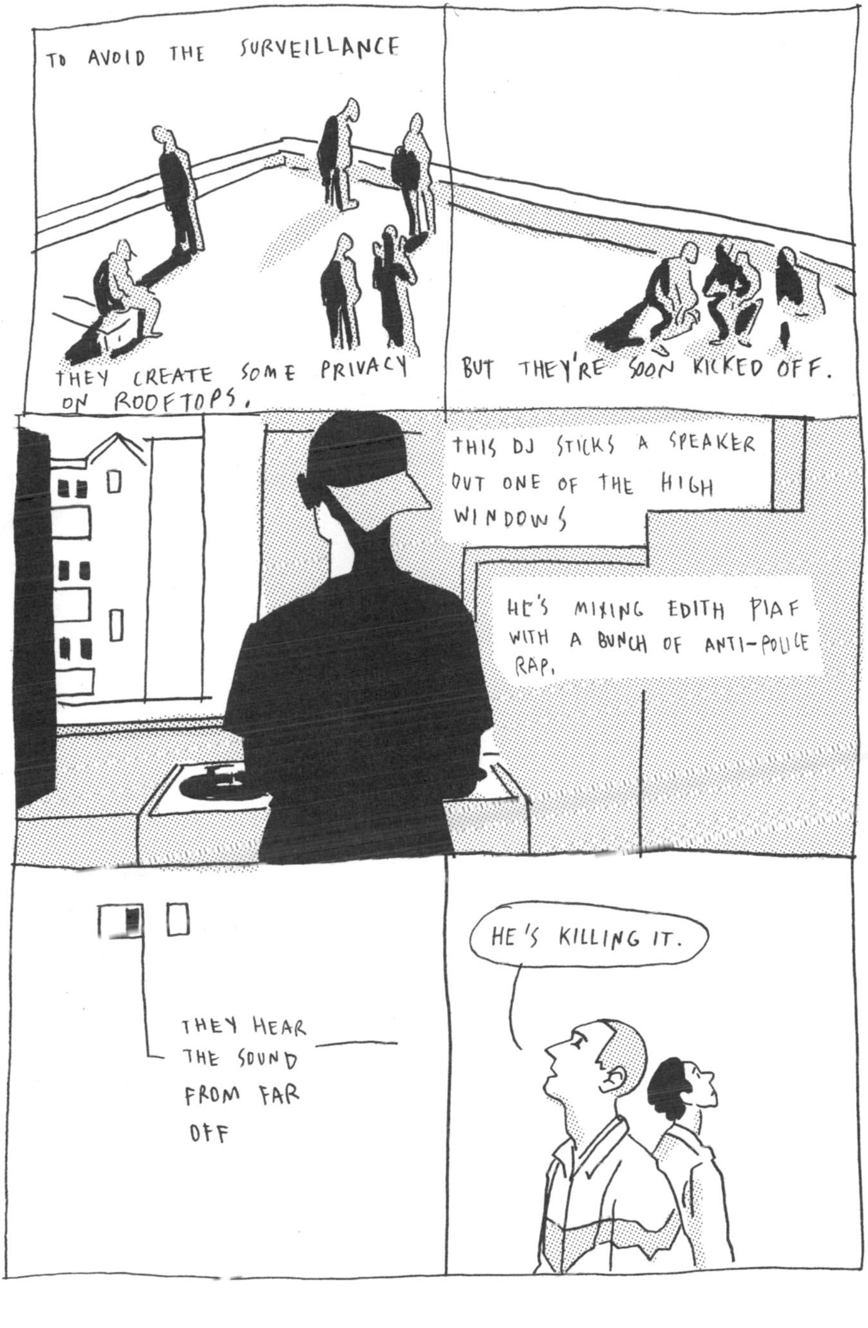
TO AVOID THE SURVEILLANCE
THEY CREATE SOME PRIVACY ON ROOFTOPS.
BUT THEY'RE SOON KICKED OFF.
THIS DJ STICKS A SPEAKER OUT ONE OF THE HIGH WINDOWS
HE'S MIXING EDITH PIAF WITH A BUNCH OF ANTI-POLICE RAP.
THEY HEAR THE SOUND FROM FAR OFF
HE'S KILLING IT.

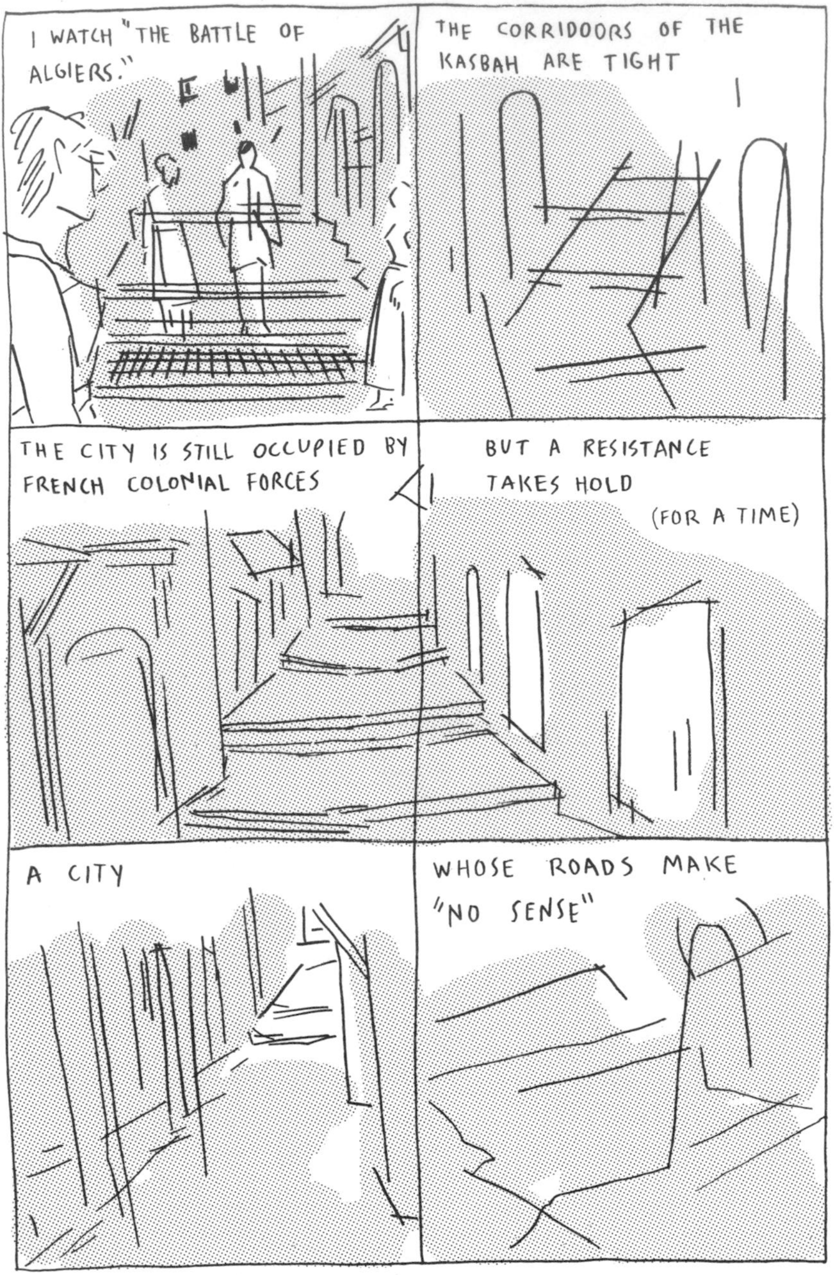
I WATCH "THE BATTLE OF ALGIERS."
THE CORRIDOORS OF THE KASBAH ARE TIGHT
THE CITY IS STILL OCCUPIED BY FRENCH COLONIAL FORCES
BUT A RESISTANCE TAKES HOLD
(FOR A TIME)
A CITY
WHOSE ROADS MAKE "NO SENSE"

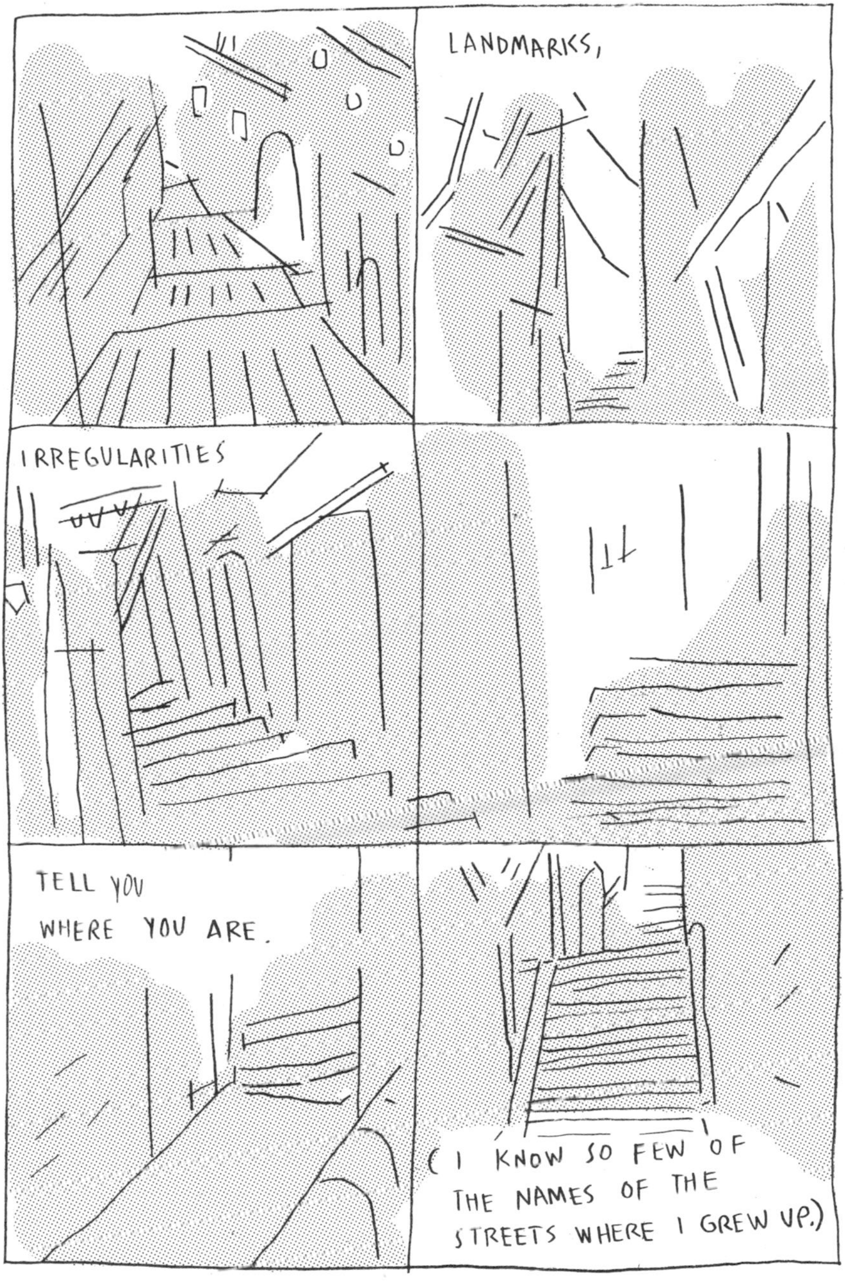
LANDMARKS,
IRREGULARITIES
TELL YOU
WHERE YOU ARE.
(I KNOW SO FEW OF
THE NAMES OF THE
STREETS WHERE I GREW UP.)

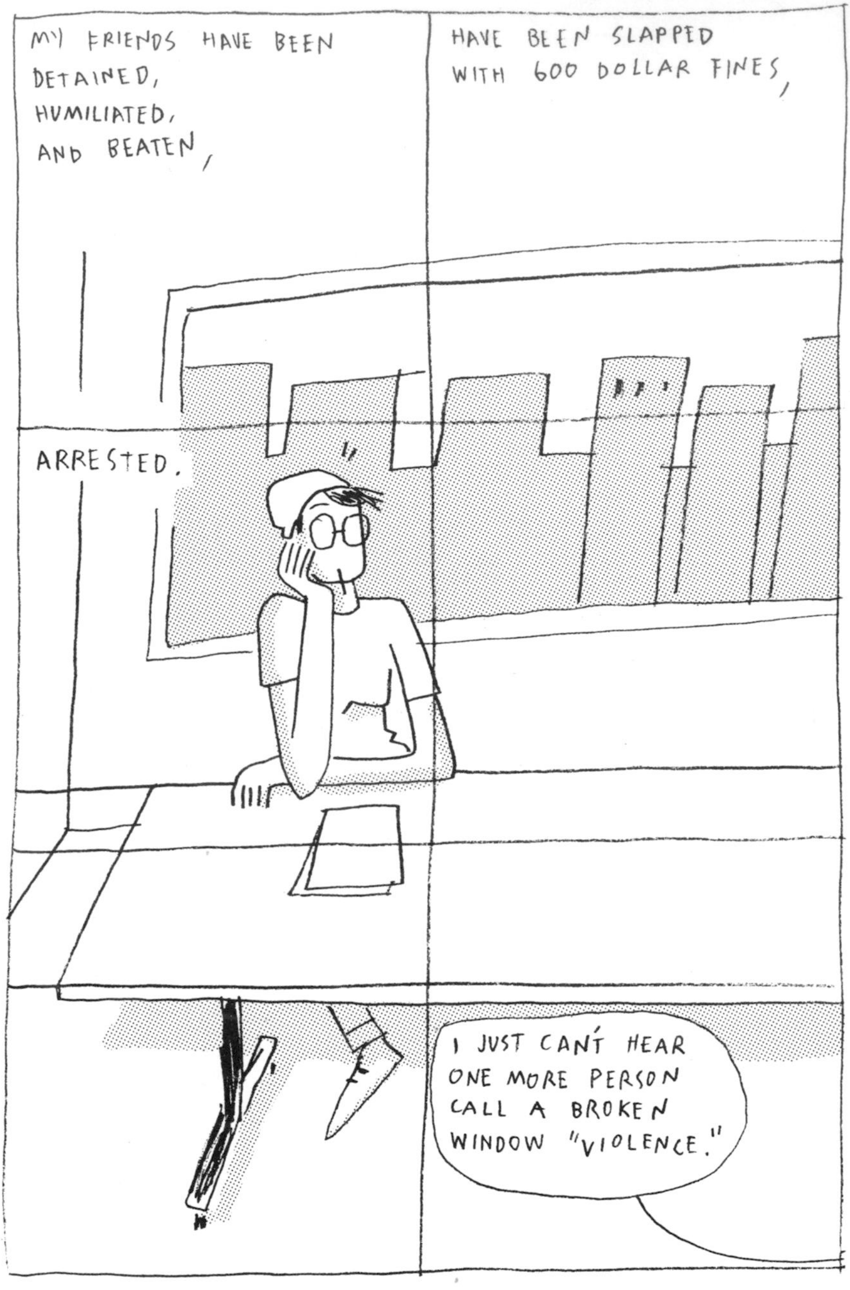
MY FRIENDS HAVE BEEN DETAINED, HUMILIATED, AND BEATEN,
HAVE BEEN SLAPPED WITH 600 DOLLAR FINES,
ARRESTED.
I JUST CAN'T HEAR ONE MORE PERSON CALL A BROKEN WINDOW "VIOLENCE."

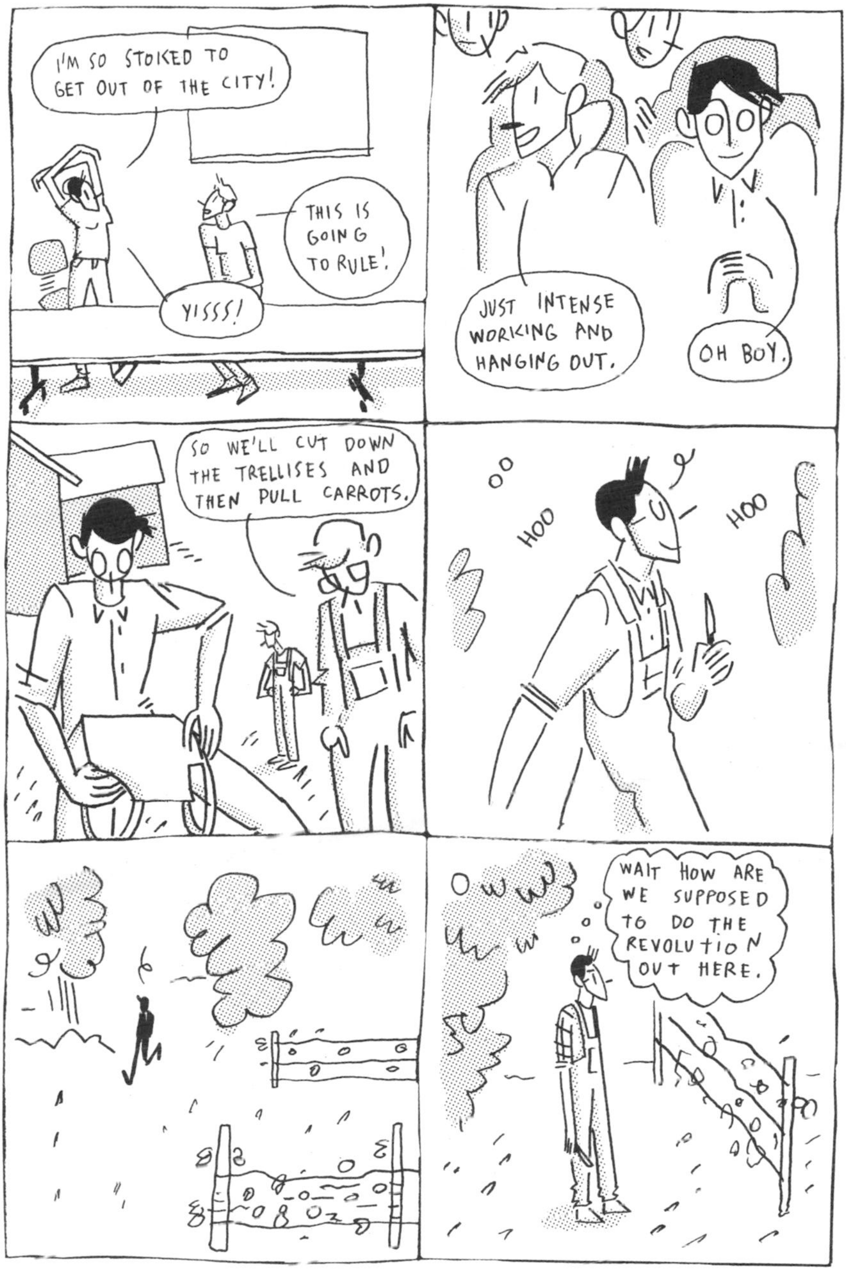
I'M SO STOKED TO GET OUT OF THE CITY!
THIS IS GOING TO RULE!
YISSS!
JUST INTENSE WORKING AND HANGING OUT.
OH BOY.
SO WE'LL CUT DOWN THE TRELLISES AND THEN PULL CARROTS.
HOO
HOO
WAIT HOW ARE WE SUPPOSED TO DO THE REVOLUTION OUT HERE.

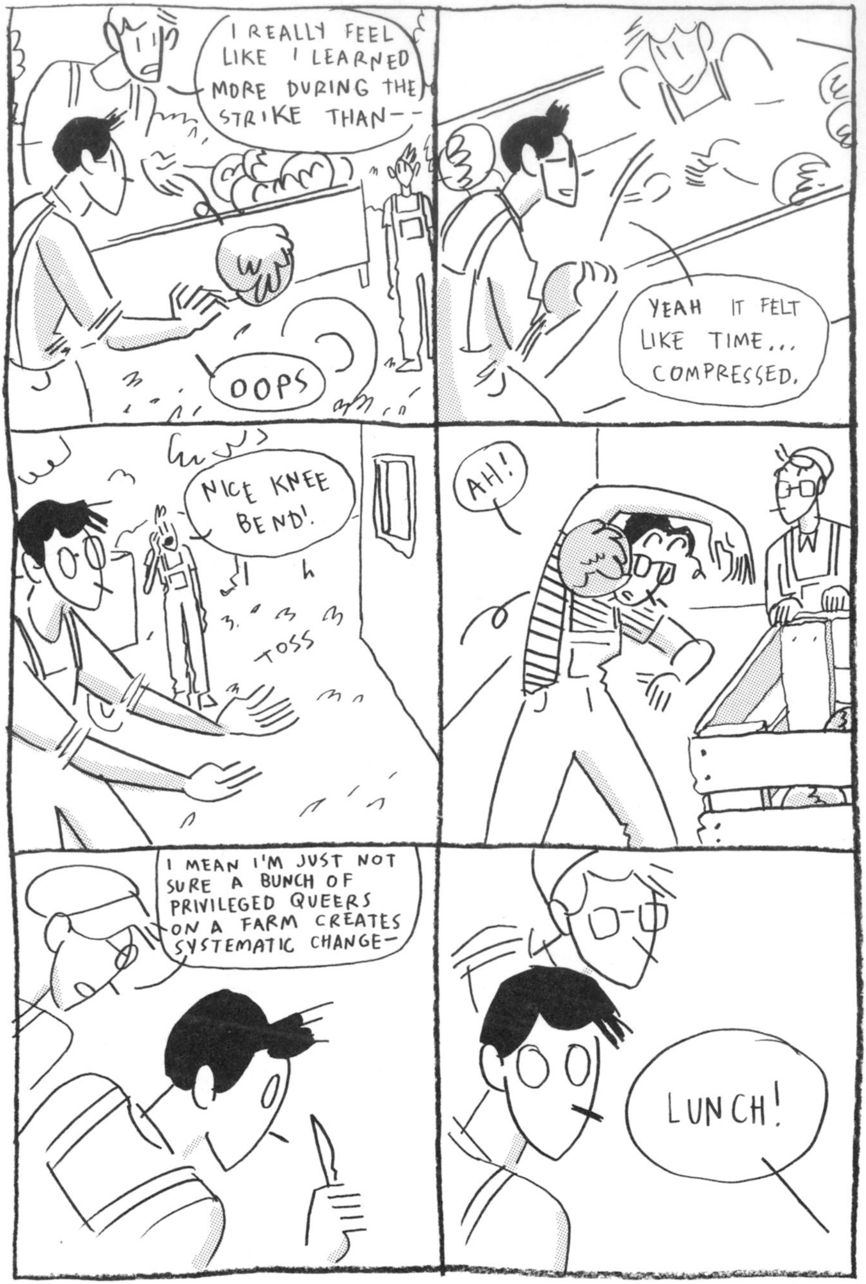
I REALLY FEEL LIKE I LEARNED MORE DURING THE STRIKE THAN--
OOPS
YEAH IT FELT LIKE TIME... COMPRESSED.
NICE KNEE BEND!
TOSS
AH!
I MEAN I'M JUST NOT SURE A BUNCH OF PRIVILEGED QUEERS ON A FARM CREATES SYSTEMATIC CHANGE-
LUNCH!

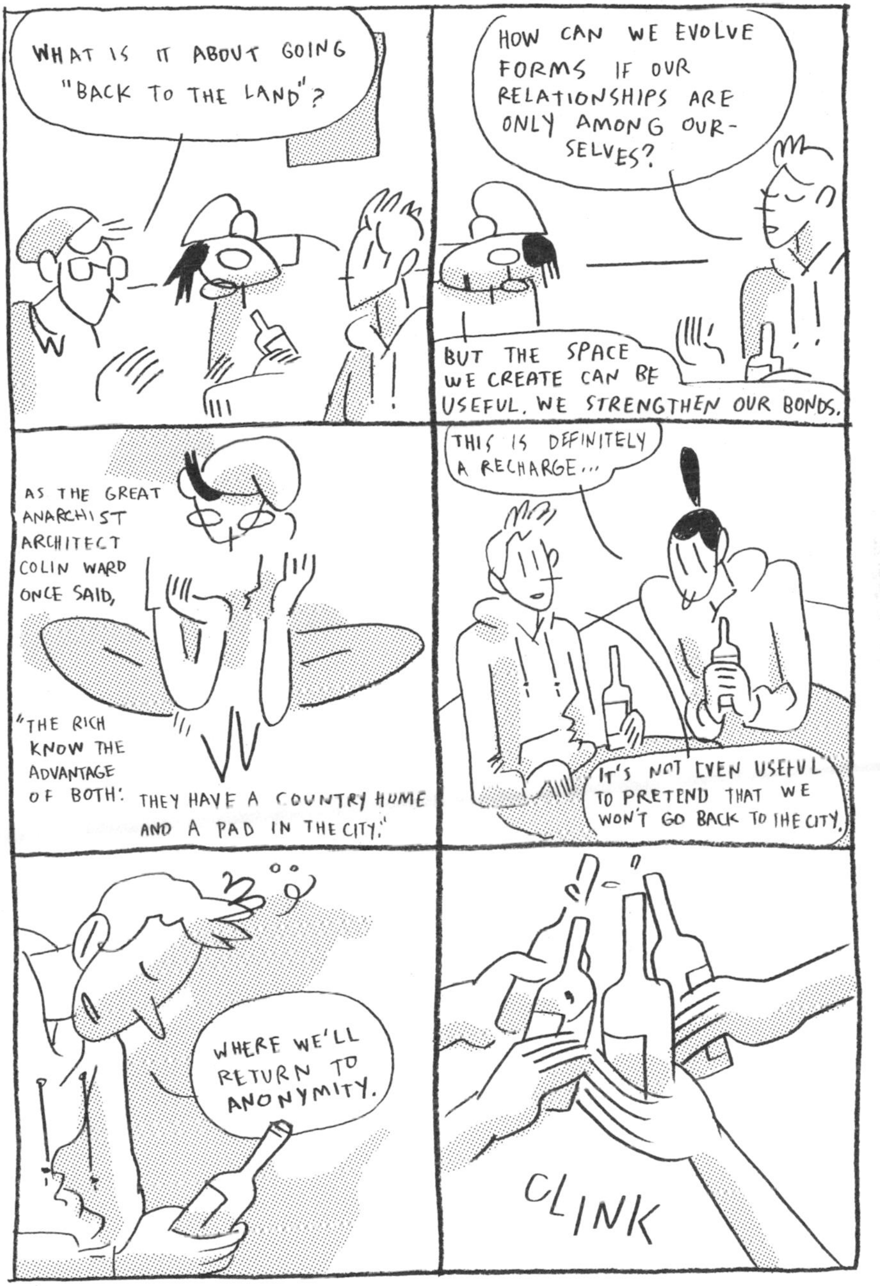
WHAT IS IT ABOUT GOING "BACK TO THE LAND"?
HOW CAN WE EVOLVE FORMS IF OUR RELATIONSHIPS ARE ONLY AMONG OURSELVES?
BUT THE SPACE WE CREATE CAN BE USEFUL. WE STRENGTHEN OUR BONDS.
AS THE GREAT ANARCHIST ARCHITECT COLIN WARD ONCE SAID,
"THE RICH KNOW THE ADVANTAGE OF BOTH: THEY HAVE A COUNTRY HOME AND A PAD IN THE CITY."
THIS IS DEFINITELY A RECHARGE...
IT'S NOT EVEN USEFUL TO PRETEND THAT WE WON'T GO BACK TO THE CITY.
WHERE WE'LL RETURN TO ANONYMITY.
CLINK

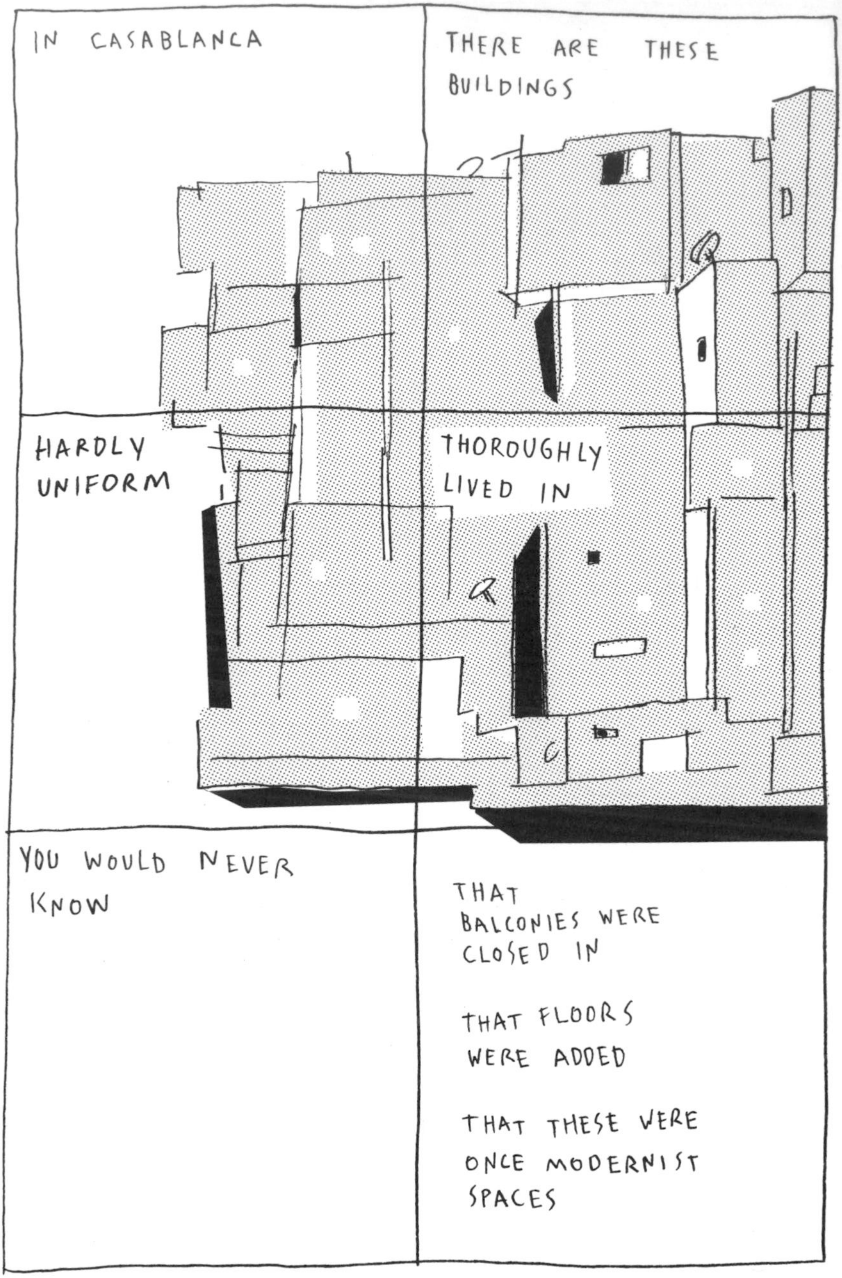
IN CASABLANCA
THERE ARE THESE BUILDINGS
HARDLY UNIFORM
THOROUGHLY LIVED IN
YOU WOULD NEVER KNOW
THAT BALCONIES WERE CLOSED IN
THAT FLOORS WERE ADDED
THAT THESE WERE ONCE MODERNIST SPACES

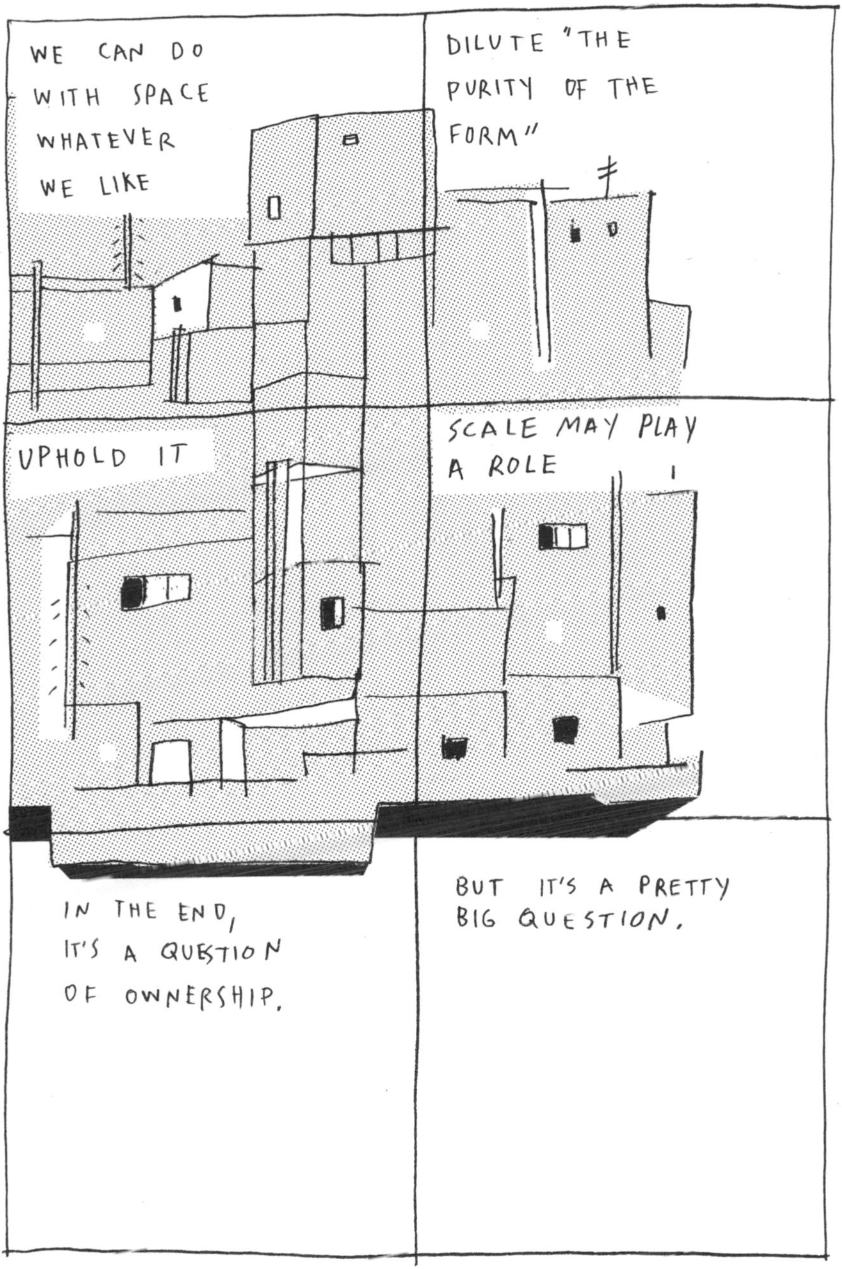
WE CAN DO
WITH SPACE
WHATEVER
WE LIKE
DILUTE "THE
PURITY OF THE
FORM"
UPHOLD IT
SCALE MAY PLAY
A ROLE
IN THE END,
IT'S A QUESTION
OF OWNERSHIP.
BUT IT'S A PRETTY
BIG QUESTION.

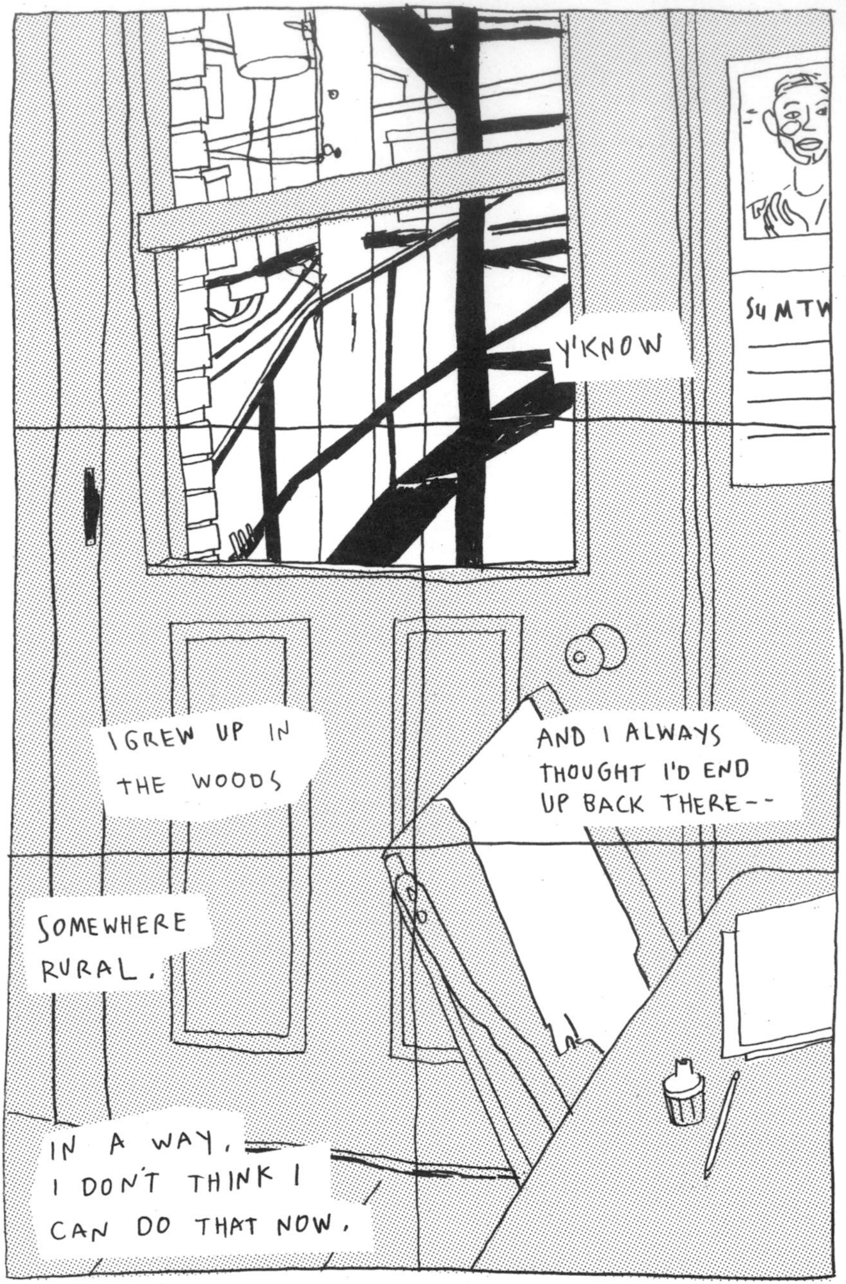
SuMTW
Y'KNOW
I GREW UP IN THE WOODS
AND I ALWAYS THOUGHT I'D END UP BACK THERE--
SOMEWHERE RURAL.
IN A WAY, I DON'T THINK I CAN DO THAT NOW.

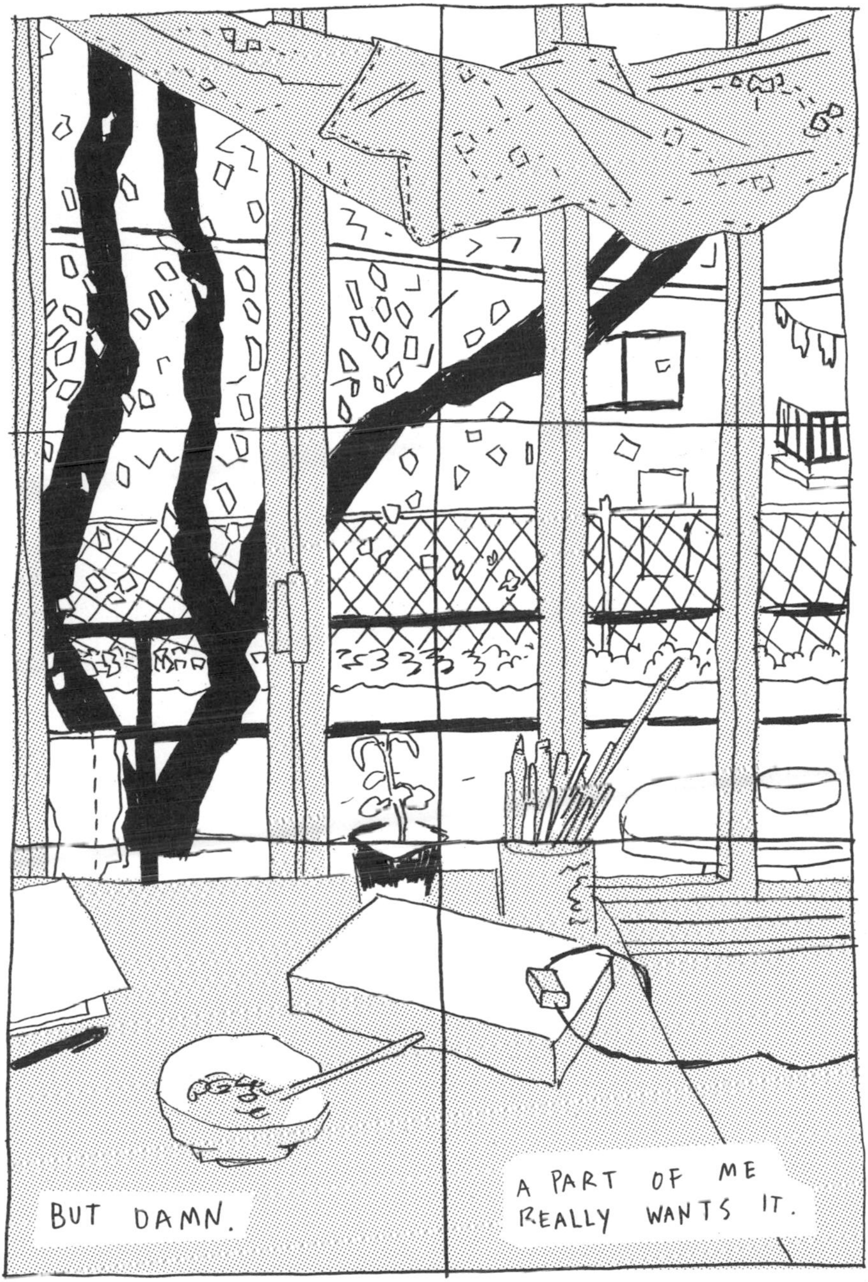
BUT DAMN.
A PART OF ME REALLY WANTS IT.

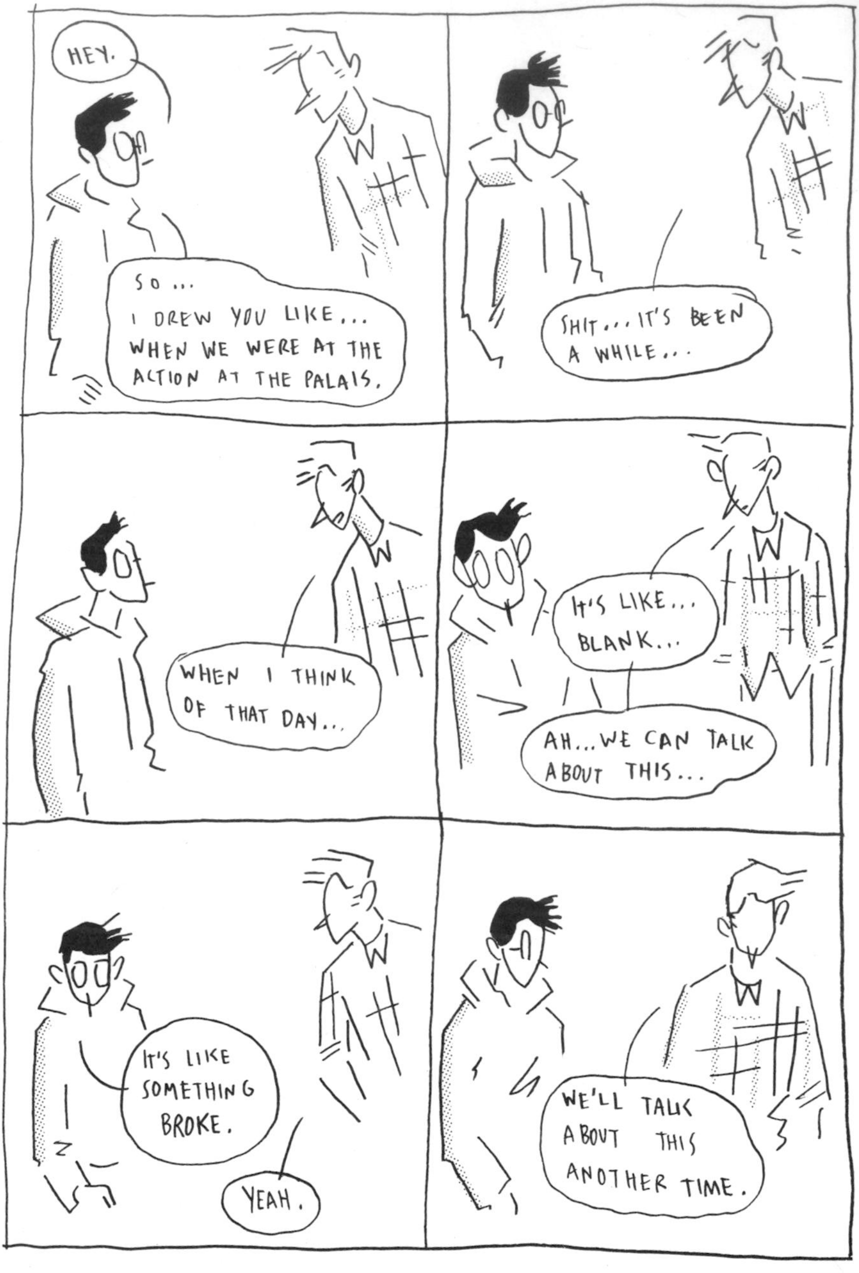
HEY.
SO ...
I DREW YOU LIKE... WHEN WE WERE AT THE ACTION AT THE PALAIS.
SHIT... IT'S BEEN A WHILE...
WHEN I THINK OF THAT DAY...
IT'S LIKE... BLANK...
AH... WE CAN TALK ABOUT THIS...
IT'S LIKE SOMETHING BROKE.
YEAH.
WE'LL TALK ABOUT THIS ANOTHER TIME.

NOTES

pp. 8-9 This is an adapted translation of a proposition passed during the general assembly the AFELLC (a student association at Montreal's UQAM, a Francophone university). The original version was republished in *On S'En Câlisse* ("We Don't Give a Damn"), a history of the student strike, written by the anonymous Collectif de Debrayage ("Stoppage Collective") and published by Entremonde/Sabotart. For a thorough militant history of the 2012 Quebec student strike, this is an excellent French language resource.

pp. 28-29 Michel Foucault, "11 January 1978," in *Security, Territory, Population: Lectures at the College de France 1977-1978*, edited Michel Senellart, translated by Graham Burchell. New York: Palgrave, 2007, pp. 1-23.

p. 31 For a description of various types of kettles, see Scott Sørli, "A Short History of Kettling," in *Scapegoat: Architecture/Landscape/Political Economy*. Issue 3, pg 10.

pp. 38-39 In 2006, Cabinet Magazine, an American magazine of "conceptual art, literature, and essays," published a translated excerpt of Bugeaud's pamphlet, *The War of Streets and Houses (La Guerre des Rues et des Maisons)*. The excerpt is introduced with a short essay by

Eyal Weizman, renowned architectural scholar, in which he gives background to Bugeaud's character, and the context in which the manual is written.

What the introduction fails to mention is that the manual was never published. Though written in 1848, it never reached the hands of the publisher - or if it did, it was repressed from ever being printed. Nonetheless, Bugeaud's exploits were notorious, and he presented his accounts and opinions in a number of texts (*The Colonization of Algeria, By the Sword and by the Plough*, etc.). In examining Bugeaud's correspondences, one finds that *The War of Streets and Houses* was quite known to his immediate circle, which was composed of many important military and political figures of the day. Victor Hugo mentions the existence of the text in a note written on January 22nd, 1849 and published in *Choses vues* (see also Jean-Louis Dufour, *La guerre, la ville et le soldat*, Odile Jacob, 2002, p. 72). Weizman does refer to Haussmann as Bugeaud's "avid reader;" and so while it's true that we may not know if he had read this particular manuscript, he nevertheless was very familiar with Bugeaud's military techniques.

Things get blurrier when we linger on the origin of the actual text which was translated. Presented under the title *La Guerre des Rues et des Maisons*, it was published by the editor Jean-Paul Rocher in 1998, close to 150 years after it was written, from a copy found by a Parisian bookseller.

Maïté Bouyssy, editor of the text, provides a few supplementary details on the genesis of this publication in a lecture given at the École normale supérieure in April, 2013 (*Guerre sociale et guerre politique dans la France de Louis-Philippe**). The historian notes that, although quite resembling the style of Bugeaud, the manuscript contains fragments which cannot be attributed to him. She also adds that the manuscript was found in the basement of a bookseller on the rue Quincampoix, and that this basement was a meeting place of members of a group called the OuLiPo (short for Ouvroir de littérature potentielle, which translates to Workshop of Potential Literature). It is Bouyssy's "unofficial theory" that, as the OuLiPo is well known for generating texts based on patterns and constraints, this manuscript may in fact

....

*<http://savoirsenmultimedia.ens.fr/expose.php?id=1304>

have been a gift from them. One wonders if Eyal Weizman and Cabinet Magazine are aware.

p. 43 Haussmann's own memoirs make no mention of the commune, although he is not the most trusted source, as his memoirs also include stories that seem never to have happened. Nonetheless, I've been unable to verify the truth of this anecdote in any other reputable source.

p. 44 David Harvey, in "Right to the City," in *New Left Review* 53, September-October 2008. 23-40. makes reference to Robert Moses, 'What Happened to Haussmann?', Architectural Forum, vol. 77 (July 1942), pp. 57–66.

p. 47 *Insurgence* is a film by anonymous members of the épopée collective of Montréal.

p. 52 *La Haine*, Mathieu Kassovitz, 1995.

p. 54 *The Battle of Algiers* (*La battaglia di Algeri*, Gillo Pontecorvo, 1966) is a film on the Algerian War (1954 - 1962) which illustrates the guerilla techniques practiced in the casbah by the Algerian resistance against the remaining French colonists. Prohibited in France until 1971, the film did not have a wide release in that country until 2004. Shown by revolutionary groups throughout the world, and at the Pentagon, where it served as an example of "how to win a battle against terrorism and lose the war of ideas." ("What Does the Pentagon See in 'Battle of Algiers'?", *The New York Times*, September 7, 2003)

p. 59 The exact citation can be found in Colin Ward, "Greening London," *Resurgence* no 181, March/April 1997.

p. 60 "Architecture Without Architects— Another Anarchist Approach," by Marion van Osten, *e-flux journal*, no 6, May 2009.

Thanks to Nasrin II for the indispensable resources.

Thanks to Julie M, Lisa M, Florent R and everyone at La Villa
for welcoming me into their space.

Thank you to the editors of the mauvaise tête edition,
Vincent Giard and Sébastien Trahan.

Thanks to Sarah A.

UNCIVILIZED BOOKS CATALOGUE

Incidents in the Night Books 1 &2 by David B.; Translated by Brian Evenson

The Voyeurs by Gabrielle Bell

Truth is Fragmentary by Gabrielle Bell

An Iranian Metamorphosis by Mana Neyestani

It Never Happened Again by Sam Alden

New Construction by Sam Alden

Amazing Facts & Beyond by Kevin Huizenga & Dan Zettwoch

Sammy The Mouse by Zak Sally

True Swamp Books 1 & 2 by Jon Lewis

Post York by James Romberger & Crosby

Eel Mansions by Derek Van Gieson

Houses of the Holy by Caitlin Skaalrud

Borb by Jason Little

Over the Wall by Peter Wartman

Pascin by Joann Sfar

uncivilizedbooks.com